Can't You See

Octavia Jensen

Written by Octavia Jensen

First edition.

Printed in the United States of America

Content Disclosure

Whitecrest is a series of interconnected standalones. They can be read by themselves, but for overarching familial storylines, it's best to read them in order.

This is an m/f romance with explicit sex, explicit language, and kinks ranging from praise to spanking.

"Love is friendship on fire."

\- Susan Sontag

ONE

Girl, Interrupting

I sat in Kale's basement surrounded by my brothers, happy that for the first time in a while, we were all together. Kale was playing the drums as his husband relaxed upstairs. Brennan sat on the couch next to me, looking content now that he wasn't surrounded by three toddlers and an exhausted wife, and although the rest of us were single, we still chose to be here on a Saturday night. This time was important to us. It always had been.

Kai had a microphone in his hand even though he wasn't singing at the moment, Archie had a guitar he was still tuning as

Sage set up his bass, and all of us pretended we didn't notice the sex swing hanging in the corner of the room or the table with restraints shoved against the wall behind us. Kale was never shy about his sex life, and we knew better than to go there unless we wanted an earful of TMI, so we acted like those things were normal decor and focused on anything else.

The rest of the basement was more welcoming. It had white lights all along the base of the ceiling, and although I knew the flood lights were a deep crimson red, I was happy he went with the brighter ones for our visit. It was like a bachelor's studio when you took out the kink and sex dungeon feels, complete with comfortable furniture and a huge TV that hung from the top of the wall.

The five extra-large pizzas we'd ordered were gone, making me wonder how the hell any of them were ever models, but I knew all of us would be working out to make up for it for the next week. Kai had probably eaten the least since he'd also ordered a salad, but the rest of us had eaten like garbage the entire night, then topped it off with booze.

I knew I wanted to go home at the end of the night, so I'd kept it to two drinks and then sat back to enjoy the show, but they were taking too damn long to play. "Think they're going to just talk the whole time, or play for us?"

"I don't know, but they'd better make up their minds soon. I can't leave Phoenix for very long," Brennan said. "Mor's got the kids right now so she can sleep, but knowing her, she'll be up in an hour wanting them back."

"Toby!" Kai yelled. "Pick a song. I hear you bitching."

"Bitching? I don't bitch." I knew it was a straight up lie, but I didn't care. "Play some Seger. Don't care which one, just get that fucking giant to stop pounding on the drums without any rhyme or reason."

Kale laughed and kept going, but when Kai turned to Archie to actually pick a song, he stopped to pay attention — and I had to admit, my brothers still had it.

It was a mark of how far Kale and Kairo had come in repairing their strained relationship that they actually took cues from each other and didn't argue once as they played a mini set, and I swore that for the first time in years, I could *see* them being twins.

Even Brennan looked impressed as they wrapped up to take a beer break until they tried to get him to play keyboard. "No. Make Tobias do it. I'm old."

"You're only two years older than me, Bror. Even if I see some grey in there already." I reached over to scratch along his scruffy face and laughed when he slapped my hand. "I'll play under one condition: twins have to take shots and Archie picks how many." They looked at me like I was weird, but in my eyes, this was free entertainment from Whitecrest's biggest names, and seeing the twins drunk was one of my favorite pastimes. "Take it or leave it."

Kai shrugged and grabbed a bottle of Absolut, then nodded to Kale. "All on you, big guy. Your husband gonna be mad if you go upstairs drunk off your giant, ridiculous ass?"

"Nah, Zack doesn't get mad … like ever. He'd just be worried since couldn't carry me to bed if he tried, but I'm fine, few shots won't hurt me. I'm bigger than all of you," Kale said confidently, but that swagger wavered slightly when Archie grinned.

"Kai, will you stay the night here or get an Uber? Our usual Uber driver is going to be drunk too, you know Sage likes to keep up."

Sage saluted us all and stole the bottle from Kai to get a head start. "Absolut-ly," he quipped. "And yes, Kai will stay here. I'm his Mom."

"Gross." Kai flipped him off but agreed to the deal, so Archie touched his smooth chin as he contemplated a number. "Since you're both technically giants, you can handle more than most of us, but

I also know you've been drinking for hours so I'll go easy … nine. Back-to-back."

Brennan and I grimaced. "I didn't expect Archie to go so hard, but I guess he's feeling froggy tonight. Sorry, guys."

Kale walked around the vodka for some white rum, then grabbed the shot glasses with a sigh, muttering something about Archie being a brat under his breath in Swedish. "Nine. Fine, but you two owe Zack an apology after I go upstairs and—"

"Shut up, nope. Don't," I interrupted, knowing that was about to cross way too many lines and give visuals none of us needed. "Take the shots, let's go."

"I just want someone to know that this is the kind of shit that gives people alcohol poisoning," Kai muttered, but he poured his first shot and slammed it back. "I really feel like I don't need you to play keyboard this bad."

Yet, he took the second shot as Kale kept up with him, then the third, fourth, and fifth ones, too. It was clear from the way he choked on that last one that he wasn't going to make it to nine, but Kale just kept going like he had a death wish, and by the ninth one he was shaking his head and staring at it like it was evil. He managed to get it down, then plopped his ass down in the middle of the floor like he was on strike. "I say we take that keyboard to the front yard and fucking break it."

"Right, 'cause that wasn't your fault at all," Brennan said with an eyeroll. "At least Kai had the good sense to tap out. Guess you only tap out when you're wrestling me."

The challenge in Kale's eyes was almost chilling. "I only tap with you because you won't stop until I die otherwise. Let's go, Brennan. Bet I don't tap tonight."

I had a bad feeling about a wrestling match breaking out downstairs, but before I could back Archie up in trying to defuse the situation, my phone rang. Even with the chaos around me, I couldn't help but smile at the interruption — it was my best friend in the world, Nila.

"You called at a horrible time, you hear them?" I knew she could hear their bickering in the background but one sniffle had me on my feet and darting up the stairs to hear her better. "Niles? What happened?"

"Oh. You're busy. I–I didn't know who else to call, there was an accident and … she's gone, T. Jackie's dead."

The despair in her tone had me slumping against the wall. "Fucking Hel," I breathed, letting my head fall back with a thud. "Where are you?"

"Home. I don't wanna be here, T. Can I come over?" Her voice wavered again as she added, "I need you."

There wasn't any situation in any world where those three words didn't make everything else disappear. Not from her lips. "Absolutely. Pack a bag, I'll come pick you up and we'll get your car another day. I'm here. I won't go anywhere but to you, okay?"

"Are you okay to drive? You're with your brothers, right? I don't want you putting yourself in danger, not after … just tell me you haven't been drinking," she begged. "Please."

"I limited myself to two drinks and the first one dried up hours ago. I'm perfectly sober." I opened the basement door and yelled I was leaving down the stairs, then waved off their million questions as I darted toward my car. I could explain it to them later.

She asked me to stay on the phone with her as she packed and I drove over, and she didn't let me hang up until she was sliding in my passenger seat and throwing her arms around my neck. "Thank you," she whispered.

"No need to thank me, Niles. I'm so fucking sorry." I squeezed her and held her as long as she needed, letting my grey shirt soak up all her tears. I didn't ask what had happened; I knew that was the last thing someone grieving wanted to answer. Jackie was her roommate and closest friend aside from me, and regardless of the cause, Nila would live with this loss forever.

It took her a full five minutes to let me go. She wiped her tears and nodded once to my shifter, which I took as my cue to drive. We stayed in silence until we were pulling into my garage.

Her movements were slow as she grabbed her bag and followed me inside, but she didn't last more than a few seconds before she was melting against me again. Her perfume filled my nose as she fisted her hands in the back of my shirt and exhaled hard.

"I just can't believe it. I don't understand."

"Do you want to talk about it?" I asked, nervous that I'd make her cry more but needing her to know I was there if she was ready.

"She ran a red light," she started slowly. "It … they said it took a while. Why'd they have to tell me that?"

"Because they're fucking sociopaths. Who the fuck would ever say some shit like that?" I calmed for a moment and sighed. "I'm sorry, was she alone?"

Fresh tears spilled as she nodded against my chest, and I'd have given anything to take her pain for her. "I need you to distract me," she whispered. "Are you hungry? Can I cook for you?"

"Cook? Really?" I smiled and ran my fingers through her hair. "I'm not hungry, but how about we make a cake together or something? We can get in PJs."

"Yes. That. Now." She composed herself a little better as she grabbed her bag again and headed upstairs to one of my spare bedrooms, and I felt so fucking bad for her I nearly followed. Instead, I rushed into my room to change, then made it back downstairs first so she wouldn't have to miss me for even a second and started pulling out all the baking ingredients.

When she came back, she glued herself to my side as we baked. It wasn't something I was unused to — for years, anytime one of us would go through something hard, it was like this. Physical contact helped ground us, helped remind us of what was real, and I couldn't stop myself from sliding my arm around her waist to hold her a little closer.

"This cake is going to be terrible," she commented. "Did we measure anything at all?"

"Nope. But come on, did any of our ancestors measure?" I knew it was going to be a disaster, but perfection wasn't the point. The point was distraction.

"No, I guess they didn't." She slid the pan into the oven and washed her hands, then smiled sadly at me. "Do you mind if I stay here for a few days? I don't really want to go back at all, but I can't afford to move right now. You people pay me well for hair and makeup, but not that well."

"Or course, as long as you need." I shrugged and reached out to wipe some flour off her chin. "If you don't want to go back at all, then don't go back. Move in here."

She laughed suddenly like she couldn't believe I'd offered, then looked at me like I was crazy when it sank in that I had. "For real?"

"Yes," I said seriously, then tried to make her smile again. "I hate living alone too, I almost got a cat after ten minutes with Millie last week."

"No, you didn't. And we're not getting a cat," she said pointedly, and wrapped her arms around me.

She wasn't the type to make a big deal out of anything at all, so I knew that was her way of saying yes.

I placed a quick kiss on her head and inhaled her scent. She always smelled so damn good, Knowing she would be here, safe, had me feeling calmer. I couldn't bear the thought of her being alone at a time like that, and maybe I happened to prefer her around me as much as possible. Either way, this felt like a good thing for both of us … even if its catalyst was a tragedy.

TWO

The Morning of Phone Calls

It took me all of four hours to realize that her moving in was a recipe for disaster. I laid awake staring at the ceiling, blinking repeatedly in hopes that I'd wake up and discover that I hadn't willingly thrown myself into the fire like that — but I could hear the television playing in the next room.

She was here.

I'd offered.

And she'd accepted.

I tossed and turned for most of the night and only woke up thanks to the smell of coffee, but she was gone when I got downstairs. All she left was a note that said she was getting some more of her things and she'd be back soon, so I poured myself a cup and called my half-sister Genesis.

We all tried to keep in contact with her as much as possible since Kale found her online, and I already knew she'd be the easiest one to talk to about this situation. She'd at least keep the teasing to a minimum. "Hey, Gen. How are you?"

"Fine, I suppose. Just got an invite to Midsummer this year, so I guess that means I made the cool kids list?"

"Hey, we invited you last year, but you had thangs to do … or whatever you Cali people say," I teased, then steered us back in a little. "I'm glad you and Mor have been talking more. She's surrounded by dudes all day."

"Your mom is a pretty cool lady. But what's up? It's not every day that I hear from you for no reason. Spill."

JENSEN

"I need a … woman's advice. That's not sexist to say, right?" I took a sip of coffee as she huffed.

"Maybe against men. You're admitting that at least in whatever area this is, women are superior. What's on your mind?"

I chuckled lightly and let her have it. "So you know my best friend Nila? Her roommate just passed away, and it's fucking tragic, but she doesn't want to live in her apartment anymore. I get it, everything there would remind her of Jackie. I wouldn't want to live there either, so I offered for her to move in. I don't regret it; I fucking love the idea, but I've uh, recently discovered I have some … unresolved feelings for her?" I covered my cringe with my hand and sighed, then nearly hung up when she waited too long to respond.

"Go on."

"'Go on' what? That's all of it." It absolutely *wasn't* all of it, so I caved instantly. "She's dating someone."

"Ah. There it is," she said, much quicker this time. "Okay. How serious is it? I'll let you decide if I'm asking about your feelings for her or her relationship."

I went with the safer option. "I'm not sure. She's mentioned him a few times and they have dinner and stuff, but she hasn't said much else, and normally she tells me everything about her dudes."

"So it's not that serious, then. Are you worried that if she's living with you, you'll see them together?"

"Yeah, mostly," I admitted. "I already have visuals of some random dude touching on her, but if I had to see it …" I didn't know how to finish that sentence, but she didn't need me to.

Her voice was softer as she said, "Why haven't you told her, Toby? I get that right this second isn't an ideal time, but … why not before?"

I shrugged even though she couldn't see me. "I was scared. I still am. I don't know how she feels and I don't want to ruin what we have. If she even got a little uncomfortable with me, she wouldn't have felt like she could come to me in her darkest moment. I mean, she's really close with her siblings and yet, she still called *me*. What if I ruined that for her?"

"What if you made it better?" she asked. "Again, I don't advise trying anything right now, but at some point you're going to get tired of torturing yourself. And if she's feeling the same way you are ... one of you will have to say something eventually. Hasn't she wondered why you haven't had a girlfriend since I've known you?"

"Probably. I just claimed I was too busy but I don't know if she believes me or not. How would you tell her if you were me?"

She made a strained noise like she was hesitant to answer. "I'm not the best person to ask about that part of it. I tend to bottle my feelings up until they explode, so ... maybe try Archie for that one."

"Archie is ... safe." My next sip of coffee was cold, but somehow that felt deserved. "When's the last time you dated someone?"

"I go on a lot of first dates. I'm not really in a place where I want to settle down, so I'm just having fun. Bet all six of you will be married before I have a steady partner," she laughed. "Maybe even one of Brenn's kids."

"Yeah right," I joined in. "I honestly thought Brennan and Kale would be last, and those assholes surprised the hell out of all of us by being the first ones."

"And you'll be next. All I know for sure is that if she does feel the same way that you do, it won't take long to find out once she moves in. Have you guys ever messed around before? Like even just for fun, or a bet, or anything?"

I thought of all the pretend kissing we'd done in front of her family and felt my cheeks heat up. "Well, kind of? Her uh — seriously, you have to promise you won't tell one brother about this, not even Archie."

"And risk missing this shit?" She clicked her tongue. "Hell no, they can pry this information out of my cold, dead hands. Spill."

I huffed an awkward laugh and rubbed the back of my neck. "Alright, fuck. So her family was up her ass about being single and dating too many guys for short periods of time, so I offered to be her fake boyfriend since they always had a million questions about our friendship too. Before this it was always purely platonic, even after I guess, but yeah. Basically they think we're a couple, and I go to all her family events and hold her hand and kiss her. We've never made out before, no tongue or groping really, just enough to be convincing."

"Yikes," she whispered. "Okay, you just … what, exactly? Kiss her like you'd kiss your wife of ten years when you're in front of the kids, or kiss her like you'd kiss your creepy aunt who insists?"

Both of those options sounded off to me. "Neither. I kiss her like she's the only woman in the world, I just do it without tongue. Over time I realized I love kissing her, and one of these times I'm going to cross a line or something. I want to kiss her even when no one else is around."

"And how does she kiss you?"

"At first, I guess like I was her husband of ten years or whatever, but lately? I kinda think she's been into them too. I grabbed her hip last time and she let out this gasp that — too far?"

"Yes and no all at once," she said after a moment. "Skip anything too graphic, but this sounds like an important detail. She seemed into it?"

"Yeah. Think if I would have kept going, she would have been all for it. Only problem was her damn mom was like right there and we haven't kissed again since."

Genesis groaned, echoing my own sentiments about that. "Okay, so … next time you kiss, do something about it. Touch her hip again. And if you need advice on what to do after that, you're really gonna have to go to one of our brothers."

"I'm not Jon Snow, Gen. I know where to put it," I deadpanned, sighing heavily as I realized how fucked I was. "Alright, not yet though. Too soon, and I don't want her to think I'm taking advantage. I just want to be what she needs for a while, then I'll go for it. Thanks, Syster."

"I still stand by the fact that it sounds the same in Swedish as it does in English," she retorted. "But you're welcome, *Bror.* Good luck, and let me know how it goes."

"I will, and it sounds a little different, ass," I smiled softly. "See you in Sweden, hope you come ready to drink."

"Wouldn't dream of coming to a family function any other way. Tell Nila I feel for her, okay? Talk soon."

She hung up and left me to my cold coffee. After chugging it down, I went to shower and get dressed for the day. I took some time to check in on the twins to make sure they were alive, but after neither of them answered the phone, I called Archie to ask him about the night I'd missed.

Unfortunately, that conversation didn't go as well as the one with our sister. The twins had gotten into a drunken argument after months without fighting, but at the very least, we were all happy they didn't throw blows. Kai still stayed the night there with Sage and Arch, but he was gone when they woke up and Zack only came downstairs to let them know Kale was alive and in bed with a hangover.

It could have gone much worse, but it also could have gone better, and maybe it would have if I'd have stayed.

It didn't matter though. Nila needed me, and I was going to be there for her as much as I could whenever I could. Archie the empath nearly cried hearing the news, but he never did well with death. One time, we'd driven past a funeral when he was in high school and the second he saw a grieving mother crying, he'd lost it too. He had no clue what happened, yet he felt that mother's pain, and ever since then, all of us had done our best to distract him if we ever came across something sad. I rushed off the phone after that so I wouldn't make it worse, texted Nila to see how she was, and then realized it had been a little while since I called my mom.

Guess this is the morning of phone calls.

I missed her though, and after she rambled on in Swedish about how I never saw her anymore, I assured her I would come by soon, but also let her know I was sure the rest of my siblings wouldn't be making it that night for dinner. "Sorry, Mor. We got a little out of hand with the alcohol, but everyone is safe."

She sighed in frustration, but I could tell their safety was what meant the most to her. "I'm getting lonely over here. Sage told me I should try The Tinder. What is that?"

I facepalmed and made an internal note to cuss out my younger brother. "It's kind of like a dating app, but not a good one for anything serious. Are you really considering dating?"

"Why not? You think I'm too old to get back out there?"

The last thing I wanted to do was deal with my mom dating shitty boyfriends, but she deserved to be happy, and if she was ready, who was I to stop her? Not to mention, she had six sons to fight her battles if someone hurt her. She'd be okay. "Of course not. I just worry about you, Mor."

"I worry about all six of you all the time, that didn't stop Kale from falling off a water tower and Sage from all of his wild adventures. It didn't stop you from climbing on the roof and falling off."

I still had the scar from that one, but I didn't need her to continue. "I got it. You're always worried, and we're still living our lives. Now it's your turn. I support you, but not on Tinder. Never take dating advice from anyone but Archie. Maybe Brennan, and me, of course. Never the other three."

"Okay, so which one if not The Tinder?"

I corrected the way she said the name then sighed in defeat. One way or the other, this was happening. I told her I would do some research on the best alternative and get back to her, then got off the phone before she could go into too many details about what she was looking for. Unless I could get Archie on board, I was sure I'd be the one to help her set up a dating profile soon, and I honestly didn't know how to feel about it. It felt like my parents were divorcing all over again, but I refused to be a child about it. Mor deserved happiness more than anyone, and I'd do whatever I needed to help … even if it meant playing matchmaker.

THREE
Crabby Pants

I turned off my 1975 Cobra with a sigh. I always hated turning off that car because it meant my drive with her was done, but to be honest … I could hear my brother a little better without the noise from the engine. "I'm not in a position to throw stones, but why are you still single again?" I had my suspicions about it, but it wasn't my place to say any of them out loud.

Kairo was five years younger than me, but something about him always seemed different. "Because I want to be," he said a little sharply. "Why the hell does everyone care so much all of a sudden? Like just because Kale settled down, I have to, too?"

"Jeez, touchy. Who else asked about it?" I took a moment to think about my five brothers, and if anyone was to grill Kai about a relationship that wasn't my mom, it would be our baby brother. "Let me guess … Archie?"

"Always Archie. He's tried to hook me up like six times in the last year alone," he admitted. "I'm not complaining about the sex, but I'm starting to feel bad about it."

"One of my siblings feels bad about sex? Are you feeling okay?" It was a joke, and not really a good one because I'd stopped my random hookups months ago. Kinda hard to care about random chicks when you knew they'd never compare to your best friend. "Kidding. Anyway, how are things with Kale? Have you seen him since the fight?"

"First of all, I don't feel bad about getting laid. I feel bad that Archie really believes he's gonna set me up one day," he clarified. "And yeah, he came over a couple of days ago. We're doing better, but we've also … got a long way to go. Can't exactly erase a decade's worth of those fights overnight."

I was glad to hear it. The whole family was sick of their fighting and it was well past time they got over their shit. "Good. He's much calmer now that he has a permanent sub, much easier to talk to, so I'm glad he's not being … *Kale* about it anymore."

"Let's not pretend I wasn't the problem. Kale reacted the way he did because I was an ass for years and tired of living in his shadow, but I'm the one who put myself there. I'm trying, Tobias. We just drank too much that night."

"You're doing great, but it takes two for a feud to go that long." I finally got out of my car when I realized I'd been stalling and started toward the house. Nila had just finished moving in and I couldn't understand why I was nervous. We'd been friends for years — we cuddled, held hands, shared a straw — why was I suddenly so damn nervous around her? To stall just a little bit longer, I stopped on the porch to keep Kai talking. "Have you talked to Fader?"

"Fuck that guy." Kai scoffed, echoing my own sentiments about our father. "No. Broke Mor's heart and ran off? Sounds like a one-way ticket out of my life. Have you?"

"No. I tried to call last week to just see if he was alive, but … no answer and he didn't call back. Glad Brennan took over Eldan International. He's doing it better anyway." Now that I'd ruined my own mood, I opened the door and stepped inside. I instantly smelled breakfast and nearly missed my brother's response entirely as I followed that scent like a dog in a cartoon.

"— I'm glad I'm just a model and don't have to deal with the shit you and Brennan d—"

"I gotta go," I rushed out. It was so strained and awkward that Nila spun around with a confused expression, like she wasn't standing in my kitchen in her panties. I heard Kai telling me I was rude as I hung up on him, then forced a smile like the situation was completely normal. "Was talking to Kai. Morning, I wasn't sure if you'd be up since you work later today."

She smiled brightly for the first time since the accident and turned her back to me again. I struggled not to watch the way the tips of her incredibly long brown hair brushed over her ass or the way that white cotton hugged her considerable curves. "It's my first official morning here. Couldn't resist cooking you breakfast, and I even made your favorite. No egg yolks in sight."

I chuckled, allowing myself to relax as things slowly drifted back to normal. They had to, or I'd have popped a very inappropriate boner. "Have I told you that you're the best lately?"

"Not nearly often enough." Nila slid a plate in front of me with an egg white omelet and Canadian bacon, then grabbed the juice from the fridge. "I do have to finish getting ready for work, but I think I've got time to eat with you. I also wanted to run something by you, if that's okay?"

"Is this food a bribe?" I joked, grinning at her as I took the juice and fighting every single urge to look at her hips.

She bit her lip, as if that made my life any easier. "Maybe. I need you to put on your boyfriend pants for me again in a couple of months. My baby sister is graduating high school finally, and you know how it goes."

"Course." I'd never deny her that. Plus, when we were pretending to be a couple around her family, it didn't really feel like it was fake. For one night every so often, I didn't have to feel like the only single person my age, and holding her hand was nice. "I love your family parties. Always plenty of good food and drinks."

And the fact that she kissed me sometimes helped, too.

"Sweet! I'll text you the date and stuff later on so you can make sure you're off.

Guess my bribe worked," she quipped, leaning over to steal a piece of bacon from my plate. "I'll be late tonight, by the way. I'll try to be quiet."

"Late? Why?" I asked, as if I had any right to know her business.

"Sage requested me for back-to-back shoots today. I don't remember all the details, but I think he said the second one might take a while … something about this particular model needing extra time in hair and makeup? I don't know."

"Sage is going to request the shit out of you unless you tell him to back off. You're too damn good and he knows it. Even the twins always ask if you're available before they'll even hear other names. I knew they'd all love your work, but damn, now you spend more time with one of my million siblings than me." I didn't realize how jealous and immature I sounded. I wasn't in a place to look at it any closer.

Nila softened. "So we'll have a date this weekend, yeah? Just you and me, like the old days. I miss you too, y'know. I could use the distraction, honestly… I'm still not exactly okay after the whole Jackie thing." She stood to come kiss the top of my head. "Do we have a deal, Crabby Pants?"

"Hey, you're just as crabby when you're tired. And yeah, deal. I'll just sleep the day away since I probably need it." I reached out to mess with her hair, but she just hummed and leaned into it.

"Do your dirty worst, Tobias. I still have to shower so it doesn't matter what you do."

"No?" I tugged slightly with my bottom lip between my teeth and when I realized what I was doing I instantly pulled my hands back and went back to my plate. "Sorry."

I knew exactly what that did for her, and watching her grip the table as she clenched her beautifully thick thighs together nearly killed me.

"Yeah, definitely shower time. Enjoy your eggs," she whispered, then disappeared up the stairs.

The sound of the water running drifted down a few moments later, and I glared down at my traitorous cock as it began to expand my slacks. I shouldn't have been thinking of her that way, I shouldn't have been wondering if she was up there with the shower head between her thighs, the thighs I'd jacked off to the thought of dying between. I shouldn't have, and yet … I was.

My cock was fully hard as I finished eating and cleaned up my mess — so hard that I had to rush to my bedroom and lock the door when I heard the water turn off.

She didn't need to see that.

Instead of doing what I really wanted to do, I forced myself into a cold shower and then slept for as long as I could. She was still gone when I awoke, but I cooked us some dinner, put her plate in the microwave and turned on *Peaky Blinders* to fill the time.

I'd seen all the episodes before, but I'd always loved re-watching shows. I was the kind of person that preferred to be home or surrounded by loved ones. I'd go on hikes with my brothers or play basketball at the local park with them, but other than that, I didn't do much, and part of me knew that was why I was perpetually single.

Not that I wanted a relationship. I didn't have the time for one with my night shifts and huge family, not to mention wanting to spend every moment I could with my best friend. I couldn't pinpoint when exactly she became my favorite person in the world, but the fact that she did wasn't lost on me … even if it might have been lost on her.

I'd met Nila in high school. She was a grade lower than me and we didn't talk much at the time; in fact, we didn't actually become best friends until well into our twenties, when we ran into each other at a bar. I remember thinking I had a shot with her — I was a Novak and under the impression that she was one of the most beautiful girls in the world. Now that I'd traveled so much of it and watched Nila grow into the stunning woman who had just cooked me breakfast, I *knew* she was.

We'd been by each other's sides through a lot of failed relationships, through heartache and loss, through my parents' divorce after Mor found out about the sister my father never told her existed. Genesis was born a few months after the twins were, and although our mom knew our dad had stepped out and broken his vow, she'd learned to forgive him with time because she didn't want us to grow up in a broken home. But when Kale found Genesis on Instagram and confirmed who she was, Mor was devastated. We all were, especially when we found out that Fader specifically told Genesis not to reach out to any of us. He basically paid her to stay hidden. None of us had forgiven him, yet sometimes I found myself wanting to check on him, and hoping that maybe he was out where Genesis was now and getting to know her. Knowing him, the latter was a pipe dream, especially since she never mentioned him.

Nila was by my side through all of it. She was even there the first time we all met Genesis, and though it was supposed to be a family thing, it felt right. It always felt right when she was around. I just wasn't man enough to do anything about it.

I couldn't lose her. I just couldn't fucking risk it.

FOUR

Things Are Kind of Hard

I took a deep breath and relaxed in my office chair as Archie walked in. He was the shortest one of us at 6'0, and in my eyes, he would always be that tiny little boy we'd all carried on our shoulders. He had the biggest heart though, and I always admired that about him. That and how damn mature he was for his age. When I was in my early twenties, I was sleeping around and not showing up for family parties because I'd partied too hard the night before. I was a horrible brother and an even worse boyfriend, and although I made a point to never be like that now that I was in my thirties, Archie had never had one of those phases.

He always put us first, always called and showed up to every gathering. He was devoted to the few partners he'd had over the years, but sometimes, I worried he would never put himself first. He'd continue to put his five siblings' love lives above his own when all he wanted was someone to call his.

"Hey, Tobes," he said. "I was about to head out and I saw you were here already. Working overtime or getting off early?"

"Off early. It's Friday and Nila's first weekend officially living with me, so we're having a date." Arch looked way too fucking excited at the word *date*, and I scolded myself for not saying it better. "Not like that. Stop."

He deflated. Normally I'd have gone into the fact that we were just friends, but for some reason, I couldn't do that anymore. "So she's all settled?" he asked, sitting in the chair across from me and making himself comfortable. "How's it been going?"

"Great. She's all moved in and walking around in her underwear so, y'know … things have been kinda hard."

My brother grimaced, not missing the accidental pun. "That's gross to know, but I'm … sorry? I don't know the proper way to say 'Sorry for your boner' to my brother."

We shared a laugh. "Nah, I was mostly joking. I love having her there, it just feels right."

That brought back his heart-eyes, and this time I just rolled mine in response. "Of course it does. I've been telling you for years that she's the one."

He had, and I was pretty much done denying it at this point. I glanced down at my phone and saw that Nila had texted, catching me completely off guard with a porn link. It wasn't uncommon for us to share those — she truly was my best friend in every sense — but like me, she was supposed to be working.

Something about my face had Archie smiling even wider, so I set my phone aside and cracked my neck. "Yeah, I guess I'm just at the point in my life where I'd rather be her best friend than not have her at all. What if I asked her on a real date and then ruined everything? Nila's never been afraid to go after what she wants, and that includes men."

"She has the same fears as you, Toby. I just know it. Just don't give up on her yet, okay? It will all work out in the end."

"Was that what you told Brennan when Phoenix moved away? Or Kale when Zack went back to wherever he was from and he was a hot mess?" I remembered those times clearly, when two of my brothers found real love and then watched it walk away. I didn't want to feel how they did in those moments, and both of them had fallen for their partners quickly. What I had with Nila was different. It wasn't some newly-formed bond — we had *years* under our belts, years where we were each other's go-to people for everything.

I didn't think either of us would be okay with losing that.

Archie simply nodded. "Yep. And was I wrong?"

Again, he wasn't. "Not everyone gets some happily ever after, Bror. You have to know that."

"I know. But that's not the case for us. It's not." He stood up completely unbothered like he had some crystal ball that told him the future.

"And what about your happily ever after, Arch? When are you going to focus on that?"

"Tonight, actually. I have a date with a girl named Dakota, and I've got a good feeling about this one." His grin was infectious, and I hoped he was right.

I told him about our mom and how she needed some dating advice, and I was pleased when he was ready to rush over then and there to help her as much as he could. We said goodbye a few moments later, and once my door was locked I went back to my phone to check out that link.

It was a good one. So good, in fact, that I found myself disappearing into my office bathroom to take care of the boner I'd neglected for days. It felt wrong in so many ways to be pulling my cock out at work, but it wasn't the first time I'd needed an emergency solo-session in there and I was pretty sure it wouldn't be the last, especially now that I had a roommate.

The woman in the video was curvy and confident, just how I loved, and she was wearing gorgeous, hot pink lace lingerie that I could've stared at for days — but when she dropped to her knees and started stroking the man's thick cock, I knew I needed to hear it.

I slipped my AirPods in just in time to hear the woman moan as she slipped him into her mouth for the first time, and when she started really sucking him off, I let my eyes close and imagined Nila. I couldn't help it; the woman in the video had the same hair color as her and everything, and for some reason, my hand felt better when it was her on my mind. I knew it could never compare to that sacred pussy I might never get to taste or feel, but sometimes my imagination was good enough to get me over the finish line feeling sated.

I could hear the guy getting close, I could hear how desperate she was to taste his load — how desperate Nila was for *mine* — and when he came, I felt my cock jerk in my hand, but for once I didn't come with him. I didn't come with him because I wasn't coming for her this time, I was going to come for Nila, the *real* Nila, and when my headphones went silent and I let myself imagine her moan when she ate her favorite ice cream, I emptied into my sink with a groan and dropped my head against the cold mirror.

It was the best orgasm I'd had in a while, but when I looked down at the mess I'd made, I couldn't stop the guilt from bubbling in my chest. I couldn't go down that road, not here at work, so I began the shame-filled cleanup process and decided I'd go find a way to distract myself.

I felt much better as I made my way downstairs to see if Nila was still around, and I was pleasantly surprised to find her cleaning up her workspace and packing up her makeup. "Hey." I kissed her forehead and leaned against her desk with a grin I couldn't mask if I tried. "Nice link, but I have to ask, were you watching porn at work?"

"Don't sit there and act like you've never done it," she whispered. "I was bored and not needed, so I snuck into one of the empty offices. I almost went into yours, but figured that was a line I'd probably regret crossing."

"Line? We have lines?" I joked, knowing that we absolutely did. Just picturing her in my office watching porn had arousal swimming through my veins again, but when I imagined her actually touching herself in there, I had to hastily change the subject. "You all ready for tonight? Might finally let you braid my hair."

She fisted a hand in it and tugged my head to the side. "Not really enough to braid, but I'll do my best. I've been looking forward to this all week."

I tried to ignore how much that tug hurt and played it off. "Me too. Movies or video games? I got the snacks all covered, I'm stopping at the store on the way home."

"Both. It's a whole weekend, right?" Nila asked. "Not like I'll have to go home at some point."

"Weekend date? You got it." I reached out to tickle her but I'd barely tapped her side when one of the models came over to interrupt us and I had to watch Nila walk away.

Sharron was gorgeous, but no matter how much she flirted with me, I felt absolutely nothing. She was a little too slim for my tastes — I preferred my partners to be plush and thick, with curves I could get lost in and soft edges instead of hard lines, and although that wasn't a secret in my world, it didn't stop some of the thinner models from trying to flirt with me. I knew it wasn't about me, it was about my name. I was attractive enough, and when I was younger, I'd soaked up all the attention I could get no matter how the girls looked — but these days, I was a lot pickier. I didn't want to settle for anything less than what I craved … anything less than *her.*

"So what are you doing this weekend?" Sharron asked, but my brother Kale came to the rescue and ensured that conversation wouldn't last too much longer.

"Yeah, what *are* your plans this weekend, Tobias?" He put me in a headlock that had Sharron giggling and backing away from our sudden wrestling match. We may have been getting older, but this kind of behavior with six brothers wasn't uncommon. Everyone around us was used to it.

Thankfully, Sharron was called away quickly, and Kale stopped almost instantly with a grin. "Figured I could save you there by kicking your ass."

He wasn't wrong on either account. Kale was bigger, younger, and faster than I was. Brennan was the only one that could outsmart him in a wrestling match. "Yeah, thanks. Was it obvious I needed saving?"

Kale snorted. "Everyone needs saving from that one. She's determined to snatch herself a Novak. She even had the nerve to ask me if I was really gay a while back." He tossed his head toward Nila and raised his eyebrows. "Go get her."

I didn't have time to unpack that before he was walking away, but all that human interaction reminded me exactly why I liked working the overnight shift. With a shake of my head, I walked over to Nila and grabbed her bag for her before she could try and lift it again. "I'll walk you out."

"How soon are you coming home?" she asked, making my stomach flip yet again when I remembered our homes were now the same place. "You done yet?"

"Like an hour. I only came in for a few hours today so I wouldn't fall behind, but this place can kiss my ass this weekend. All yours, Niles." I grinned as we started walking. "Chinese good for tonight or should we cook?"

"Chinese is great, and don't skimp on the wontons. I'd cook for you but I don't want you getting spoiled." She stuck her tongue out at me and opened her car door, then slipped inside. "Don't be late."

"Wouldn't dream of it." I set her bag in the backseat and watched her drive away, then went back to work.

I wouldn't admit it to her, but I didn't last very long knowing she was at home waiting for me. I ducked out at the first opportunity and then called in a takeout order on my way to the store, ensuring I got extra wontons for her and enough of everything else to last the weekend. After all Nila had been through the last few months, I had to show her that the rest of the year would be better … and if that also meant she finally *saw* me, then I'd be pretty damn okay with that.

Don't get your hopes up, Tobias. Archie's been wrong about love working out before.

FIVE

Brains, Boners, and Chinese Food

All her favorites from her favorite Chinese restaurant, check. Weird spicy-sweet chips she likes, check. Chocolate everything like she loves, check.

I made sure not to forget her popcorn and M&Ms and drove home feeling confident I had everything to make for a good, relaxing weekend. My hands were full when I walked into the house, but she was right there to help me with everything and then ordered me to shower while she dished everything up.

I came down about ten minutes later in my Loki pajamas, finally getting a good view of her adorable Harry Potter PJs as she handed me my plate. Short shorts and a tank, both white with little gold Snitches and lightning bolts on them — they hugged her body in all the right ways and teased me just a little too much. "Nice," I said. "Let's do a scary movie first while we eat."

She raised an eyebrow at me as she sat down and curled her legs under her. "Scary? You?"

"Hey, I do scary sometimes. You're the one that's gonna end up on my lap." *Which would be bad these days seeing as you constantly give me a boner, and I'm pretty sure your boyfriend wouldn't be too happy about it.*

"As long as you're aware of that." She reached forward to swipe the remote off the coffee table and flipped through our choices, then picked one that looked like it would scare the shit out of both of us. "This good?"

"Yup. Devil shit, the worst kind of movie." I scooted a tad closer and started eating, loving how natural things felt with her.

It only took her twenty minutes to jump so suddenly that the rest of her food ended up on the floor. She cussed loudly and picked the container back up, but she had sweet and sour sauce all over her lap.

I was laughing so hard I had to pause the movie, but I really did feel bad. Once I'd gotten her some paper towels and helped her clean, I shook my head and tried not to laugh more. "Your white PJs look like a crime scene now, Niles."

"Fuck off. Could've happened to anyone," she said, fighting a grin. "Guess I should go shower, huh? I'm all sticky now."

"Yeah, probably." I imagined myself licking the sauce off her thick thighs and then backed away. "I'll keep it paused and stay close so you don't have to be scared."

Her eyes widened a little. "Oh, hell. The last thing I should be doing is showering.

That's like move number one for getting killed in a horror movie."

"You're not wrong there. Maybe just change and wipe off your — your —" I pointed at her lower body, unable to even say the damn word because I knew I was seconds away from getting hard.

"Thighs? You feeling okay, T?" She held the back of her hand to my forehead and laughed beautifully, then turned to dash up the stairs. "Be back in five!"

"Yup, I'll be right here." I scratched my head as she disappeared and then cursed myself for being fucking awkward. I was just glad I *didn't* get a boner.

She came back down a few minutes later in fresh pajamas and smelling like a dream — then sat right next to me and threw those thighs over my lap. "Okay. We can keep going now. Nothing ate me up there."

"I was listening closely. Would have been up there in seconds if any demon kids got you." I pressed play and started massaging her feet without realizing, but this was normal behavior for us.

Another twenty minutes in, she was completely in my lap, swearing at the people in the movie making all the wrong decisions. I had to force her to drink water, but having her so close helped a lot. Her scent filled all my senses and her skin was so soft that I completely forgot to be scared.

All I felt was her.

When that movie was over, she got up and shook off the nerves. "Okay, maybe something lighter next, but we should build the fort first just in case one of us passes out."

"You got it." We got to work, glancing at each other every so often and smiling like a couple of high schoolers. I couldn't pinpoint why, but I also didn't allow myself to look any closer at it. She was here, and even if that was all I would get, I'd still be happy.

"So romcom, raunchy com, or … fantasy?" I asked when we were about finished.

"If you're offering a *Lord of the Rings* marathon, I'm not going to say no. But I'm okay with any of it. I picked the last one, so surprise me," she said, tossing a couple of pillows under the sheet we'd stretched from the back of the couch to the wall above the television.

We took a quick break to go get ready for bed, then crowded under that sheet with popcorn, wine, and chocolate. I went with a romcom since we needed the laughs and the cheesiness that came with them, and *Lord of the Rings* would have kept us up the entire night.

Even though the movie wasn't scary, I could still feel her gravitating close to me, like there was some invisible pull between us that we'd fought off for so long it was becoming more difficult by the day. Or maybe it was all in my head, I wasn't entirely sure.

"Get over here," she mumbled toward the end of the movie. She was half-asleep already and reaching back to pull me closer, closer until I was pressed up against her back and wrapping an arm around her. "Better. Night, T. Can't keep my eyes open."

"Sleep good," I mumbled, pressing a kiss to her shoulder and relaxing completely. This wasn't outside of the norm for us, regardless of all the feelings warring inside my body. We needed this contact and we needed it from each other, because at the end of the day, we both knew we were safe here. And sometimes … that had to be enough.

~

I woke up the next morning to find her drooling all over my chest. My shirt had a little wet spot that was only getting bigger. She was so warm, so comfortable that I couldn't bring myself to move, and yet when I felt what was between my legs I knew I had to. I slipped out from under her as gently as I could, but it wasn't enough to stop her from opening her ice blue eyes.

"Good m— oh," she said quickly, sitting up as I tried to hide my morning wood. "So you're happy to see me, huh?" she teased.

I huffed, pressing it down as much as I could with a blush. "It's a side effect of waking up. But yeah, course I am. Nothing to see here." But there was — it was probably the first time she'd seen me with a full, raging boner, and I cursed my bladder for ruining that sleepy daze in her eyes. She was wide awake now.

"Guess it's true what they say about the Novaks. You're all … gifted." She cleared her throat and squirmed a little, but played it off by getting out of the fort and heading for the kitchen. "Wontons for breakfast?"

"Yup. Sounds great, I'll just go … take care of this. But wait, who says that exactly?" I was grinning playfully, letting her know I was absolutely looking for the confidence boost, and she shrugged one shoulder like it wasn't a big deal.

"Everyone. All the people you six have messed around with, the girlfriends and boyfriends I've known, every tabloid in America … Phoenix and Zack."

"For the record, my number is lower than most of my brothers … if that counts for anything." I rushed off to take care of my problem and then brushed my teeth before making my way back down to her.

She was eying me like that little detour meant nothing. "Why is that, by the way? Your number being lower than your brothers'."

I shrugged. "Because they're sluts. Two of them are hitched now so they aren't anymore, but Sage is still a slut. Don't really know much about what Kai's been up to in that department, but Archie's probably been with less people than I have. I don't actually know my number though, is that something people actually keep track of?"

"Yeah, unless it's too high to count." She watched me. "Is it too high to count?"

I looked around the room as I gave it some serious thought and realized that it probably was. "Maybe. Not lately though." I met her eyes for the briefest of seconds and then made my way to the fridge. "What about yours?"

"I'm not exactly secretive about it. I'm pretty sure I've told you about all of mine," she said conversationally. "All twelve of them."

She had. "I didn't know I knew about all of them but I do remember twelve." *Not like I was counting or anything.* "Is over a hundred a lot?"

"Little bit, yeah." She bumped me with her hip as she put the wontons in the microwave. "Just glad none of them stuck, honestly. Most women won't care for our friendship."

"I know. Same with men, though. People don't like to share unless they *really* like to share. I mean, I don't even like sharing you with your other friends and family."

Her eyes danced a little. "I've noticed. You were a little too eager for me to move in here instead of with Jackson," she said. "Not that I really wanted to live with him, anyway. It's way too soon."

"I have more room here. I wanted you to be comfortable when you got home from work and I knew you'd be happiest here." My motives may have truly been selfish, but I really did care about her happiness. "Plus, now I always know where to find you when you ignore your phone for a day."

Nila hummed, pulling the wontons out and biting the tip off of one. "If I didn't know any better, I'd say you were one of those crazy possessive boyfriends. Maybe that's why no one sticks around."

The possession for her that ran through my veins in that moment was so overwhelming, I nearly kissed her. She wasn't wrong, and I was completely unable to deny it. "What can I say … what's mine is mine."

"Well right now, 'what's yours' is starving, so maybe we should order in and eat breakfast on the floor. I still need to braid your hair."

What's mine … love the way that sounds. "Sounds like a good plan to me, but I'm braiding yours too." *I have to fucking tug it. I need to hear the sound it causes with me behind you.* "Eat. 'What's yours' is starving too."

She ordered breakfast for us and we sat too close while we started that LOTR marathon and ate, but I chickened out of letting her braid my hair. The moment she pulled a little too hard, I grunted in pain. "The hell was that for? You mad at me for something?"

"What? No. Your hair is too short to braid properly, if you think it hurts now … it won't get any better. Wanna switch?"

"Well, fuck." I rubbed my head and moved away. "Yeah, let's switch. If braiding hurts that bad, no way you last either."

She snorted. "Good luck hurting my head. My hair is down to my ass, which you don't get with a sensitive baby scalp like yours," she teased, kissing the top of my head before climbing over me to switch spots. "Let's hope you're better at giving than receiving."

"That's been proven—" I got comfortable behind her and then leaned in to whisper — "time and time again." I got to work on her hair, and though I didn't have a clue what I was doing, that wasn't going to stop me in the slightest. "Does it have to be in three sections?"

"Babe, do you know anything about braids? Yes, it needs to be in three sections." She wiggled a little bit. "So does that mean you're terrible at getting blowjobs or you're just really good at eating out?"

"Both, I guess. My first priority is getting her off with my tongue, and I normally lose control when she blows me. Not everyone likes it rough." I tugged a little to test her, and I wasn't sure if the moan she let out or the way she clenched her thighs together was more satisfying, but the combination was beautiful.

"Some of us do," she whispered. "You'll find someone someday who will let you fuck their face until they pass out on your cock. Don't worry, T."

"Fuck," I whispered sharply. "You can't … fucking Hel. You can't make that noise and say something like that, this one is your fault."

She turned slightly to see the way I was tenting my pajamas, then grinned. "I'm not sorry. That's what friends are for, right?"

"Yep. Braids, boners, and Chinese food. We got our own BBC going on here, Nila. Stop staring at it." I grabbed a pillow and blocked it from her view, so she hummed and settled back between my legs.

"Then go on. Three sections, and you just sort of loop them over top of each other. I really don't care how it looks, it just feels good to be touched."

"You got it, bossy." I smoothed out her hair and took some time massaging her scalp before I followed her directions. Part of me wondered why Jackson wasn't the one touching her right then, but the swell of pride and jealousy in my chest ensured I pushed him from my mind quickly. "Honestly, feels good to touch too. Think that's why people are sluts … that deep, ingrained need to be touched that lives inside of all of us. I'll be that person for you, Nila. Whenever you need me."

She was silent for a moment, then whispered, "I can be that for you too, T. All you have to do is ask."

I wanted to. I wanted to tell her I needed to touch every single inch of her skin until I could make a map of it blindfolded … but I didn't. Instead I kept going, making a complete mess of her hair, and after we took a photo of us together we cuddled some more as the movie played.

For the first time in our friendship I had no clue what the next day would hold, and I suddenly knew exactly why two of my brothers were Doms.

Not having control was fucking terrifying.

SIX

Don't Be Barbaric

"You look beat, Niles. Need a famous Novak massage?" I smiled at her, trying not to show how badly I needed to touch her.

"How am I supposed to say no to that?" she asked, moving a little closer to me. "I'm convinced you've got the best hands I've ever felt."

"You're not wrong. And you can feel them any time, any place, sweetheart. Just give me those adorable puppy eyes and you got it." I reached behind her and started rubbing, loving how she melted into me and let out a soft moan.

I was just finding a rhythm when she gasped and whipped her head toward the clock. "Oh, shit! I have to get dressed. Move, T, sorry!"

She dashed up the stairs, leaving my hands extended in the air in shock. She'd never been strong enough to walk away from one of my massages. I frowned at the stairs and let my hands drop into my lap as I waited, trying to remember what plans she had and raking through the conversations we'd had that evening. Absolutely nothing stood out — which meant she was most likely going out with fucking Jackson.

I glared at the dual Xbox controllers I had thought we would be using together, then slumped into the couch as I waited for her to come down. When she did, her outfit confirmed my suspicion. She was wearing another dress — this one as deeply green as the jealousy I was feeling

— and the heels she had on made her almost as tall as me.

Almost.

"Do I look okay?" she asked, twirling around, and I nodded in spite of my inner turmoil.

"You look beautiful. You always do," I assured, walking over to get a better look at her curves in what was suddenly simultaneously my favorite *and* most hated dress she owned … because it wasn't for me. "Jackson?"

She nodded a little shyly, which was unlike her. "Yeah. He should be here any minute actually. Do you want to meet him? "

No. "Yeah, what date is this again? I think it's past time he meets the number three guy in your life. Your dad and brother are lucky there's blood relation or I'd snatch up that number one slot." I forced a smile for her and looked down at my bare chest and grey sweatpants. "Should I go find a shirt?"

Her fingertips brushed my skin. "Nah. And it's cute you think you're number three." She grinned playfully and spun away from me, then opened the door a split second later when someone knocked. "Date eight, T. Meet Jackson."

He walked in, and I couldn't stop the straightening of my spine as I approached him, nor the primal, possessive emanations my body sent straight through our joined hands so it was tangible between only us. She was mine, and Jackson needed to know it. Jackson with his thicker beard, annoyingly green eyes, and muscular upper body that stretched out his shirt. *Fucking tool.* "Date eight, huh? Thought he made it to ten by now. You know leg day should never be skipped right, Jack?"

"Tobias Novak. You're exactly as … well, let's just say you're exactly who I thought you'd be." He shook my hand a little harder, then let go to grab Nila's face and kiss her deeply. I huffed and backed away, using all my strength not to punch him in the face or take his bait.

The blatant reminder that she *wasn't* in fact mine helped. "I'll take that as a compliment. Have fun tonight, Niles. I'll be up when you get home."

She waved to me with a frown as he led her toward the door without another glance my way, and I heard her out on the porch asking him why he couldn't get along with me for her sake.

I spent my alone time playing a game and sulking, angry at myself for not punching him, yet proud of containing the urge for Nila's sake. The last thing she needed was me going all macho on her at a time like this, but knowing that didn't make it any easier.

I found myself checking the time nearly every hour, and to torture myself even more I started to picture what they were doing. Was he touching her? Making her feel good in ways I never had? Ways that I might never get to try?

I hated myself for it.

I took a long shower to pass the time and ate nearly all the leftovers in the fridge before I gave up on everything and sat in silence.

When she finally got back home, I couldn't stop myself from standing and moving toward the door. I knew there was a very real possibility that he would be with her, but I was well beyond caring. "Niles?"

She looked half upset and half relieved to see me, and she walked in alone and closed the door behind her. "There won't be a date ten. Or a date nine, for that matter."

I was glad I was strong enough not to smile. The last thing I wanted to do was hurt her any more than she'd already been hurt, and when I opened my mouth to speak, my stomach dropped as I waited for an answer. "What happened? Did he do something to you?"

"No. It was the same story as always. He was too insecure to deal with me living with a half-naked Novak, and I told you years ago I'd never let a man come between us. I meant that." She set her purse down and kicked off her heels, leaning over to pick them up. "You have a tub in the bathroom in your room, right? Mind if I take a bubble bath?"

"Course not, I'll go set it up for you. Mind if I keep you company? I'll stay on my bed where I can't see you, I just want to be there if you want to talk." I moved behind her to help her unzip her dress, my breath hitching in my throat as her skin was exposed and I moved back around to compose myself.

"Sounds like a plan. I'll get my things."

Nila flashed me a tight-lipped smile as she headed upstairs to the bathroom she normally used, and I barely had time to get the bath filled before she was walking in wearing nothing but a dark grey towel.

My eyes dropped naturally, lining her body shape slowly and deliberately and when I made it to her face she was watching me. "Sorry about Jackwagon," I lied.

"I'm not." She slowly walked past me until she was out of my line of sight, and I heard that towel hit the floor a moment before the water splashed lightly. "We're a package deal, T. Someday, someone will realize it."

I sure as fuck hope not. "We are." I sat on my bed and laid back to stare at the ceiling, because when I glanced over and saw that towel on the floor, my cock swelled. *It's a fucking towel for Christ sake. Pull your shit together.*

The shuddering breath I released was so loud I feared she'd hear it. "So far, none of the women I've dated understood either." Just thinking of other women helped the throbbing in my sweats cease. "They all wanted to come before you, and I just couldn't fucking do that. You'll always be my number one girl, Nila." *Even if you marry and slowly leave me behind.*

"And you're my number one guy." The water sloshed gently again. "That's why I laughed before I left. I love my dad and Clay, but … this is different. You're different."

I smiled like some high school boy who'd gotten paired with his crush for a project. "I'm not going anywhere, okay? No matter what, you got me." I didn't know why I went there in that moment, but being able to hear her and not see her helped in a way I didn't understand. I felt open and raw without an ounce of vulnerability. It was calming. "Remember when we got back in touch? When we hung out at the beach and Sage and Kale got so drunk I had you hide me so I didn't have to babysit for a while?"

"Yes. That was the first time we fell asleep cuddling," she said quietly. "We found Sage under a pile of naked people who didn't even speak the same language he did."

I laughed, shaking my head at the memory and sort of in awe one of my siblings never caught anything. Or if they had, they never told me. "Did I ever tell you I thought that was a date?"

"It was," she laughed. "You just forgot to ask for a second one."

I almost asked her. I almost threw all caution to the wind and told her I wanted a second date, and a third date, and a hundredth date. I wanted her all to myself so badly it hurt, but the timing felt off. Asking her out now of all times, after she'd just lost a friend and broken up with a guy … it felt barbaric. "I guess being a dumbass isn't a new thing for me. Do you want some wine?"

"Abso-fucking-lutely. Please."

I snuck a glance and saw her dragging those bubbles up her bare arm and had to force myself from the room. I was hard again, and this time it didn't seem to want to go down. I thought of that day on the beach, of how we cuddled and I thought I'd be fucking her but instead I let her fall asleep against me and held her. It was strange for me, but I thought of that moment often and it was worth the blue balls that came with it.

I took longer than I should have to bring her a glass, and when I walked in and saw her chest covered in bubbles I lost all the progress I'd made out there. I was too fucking horny for this. "It's your favorite."

"I don't deserve you." She took it with a genuine, warm smile, then nodded to the floor by the shower just a few feet away. "You don't have to go. I'm not embarrassed."

I shrunk down to the floor like the lovesick dog that I was and stared down at the glass in my hands before taking a long sip of scotch. "Don't know what I'd do without you, Niles. I know the things I've been through don't compare to yours, but I'd be fucking lost without you."

"Well … then here's to being lost together." She leaned forward to clink our glasses, then tilted her head back to sip. I watched with hooded eyes as the water clung to her neck and the top of her chest, making my breathing get more ragged by the second, and before I knew what I was doing I stood up and shot back my drink. "Be right back."

I rushed out so hard I could hardly walk, without any intentions of refilling my glass and all of the intentions of beating my meat. Based on how hard I was, it wasn't going to take me long, so I shoved down my sweats and fisted my overheated, throbbing cock, moaning the second my cooler hand made contact. I jacked off without any finesse or rhythm, solely for the purpose of coming into my hand, and when I remembered she was naked inside *my* tub, I came almost instantly. I came with her name in my throat and her face in my mind, long strips of white audibly splattering to the floor, and when I realized what I'd done I wanted to slap myself.

My floor was a mess — I was a mess, and she was still naked upstairs waiting for me.

I cleaned up as quickly as I could and went back to her with red cheeks and a still-empty glass. She knew what I'd done, and I knew she knew it … I just didn't know what the fuck to say.

"Been a while, huh?" she said, more gently than I deserved. She was already out of the tub with those Snitch pajamas on again, looking comfortable and relaxed, like she wasn't judging me at all. "I know the feeling. I never made it that far with Jackson."

My gaze darted up in surprise, but all I saw in her eyes was honesty. "His loss."

I couldn't place the small smile on her face as I watched her leave, but there wasn't a question in my mind anymore. I didn't just have feelings for my best friend — I was in love with her.

SEVEN

Unresolved Sexual Tension

I felt like a coward as I straightened my tie in the mirror and grabbed my coat. It was the night of her sister's graduation party and I was about to spend the next few hours holding Nila's hand, pretending to be her man, and in the end, I'd even go home with her. Yet she wouldn't be mine.

"Ready?" she called, knocking lightly on my door, and when she opened it, I nearly couldn't breathe. She was wearing a baby blue V-neck summer dress that hugged her body in all the right ways, and her insanely long hair was falling in curls over her shoulders. "Look at you. I knew I picked the right guy to be my fake boyfriend."

"Right?" I chuckled, spinning around for her before strutting forward. "You got good taste, just not as good as mine. Love this color on you."

"Yeah?" she asked, spinning for me once then grabbing my hands to make me dance with her. "So you won't mind loving all over me today so my asshole family doesn't grill me about why I'm chronically single?"

"Course not, everyone always thinks we're a couple anyway. It's easy with you." I let my hands fall to her lower back and lost myself in a sea of blue. "Will you dance with me there?"

She nodded as she bit her lower lip. "Knowing Juliet, she'll insist on having music and a dance floor, so yes. Now let's go, we're gonna be late."

I opted for the Tesla this time and played her favorite band the whole drive. Our personal car concert helped ease the nerves, and when we arrived, I tossed my arm around her shoulders and leaned in to kiss her cheek. "Just getting in the zone before we get in."

I grinned cheekily and opened the door, then followed her to greet her parents, siblings, and aunts and uncles. I'd been doing this with her long enough that I knew all of their names and the things they liked to do, but I'd never get used to the way she laced her fingers with mine and pouted her lips for a kiss after saying something cute about me and how well our "relationship" was going.

The desire for it to be real had me leaning in quickly and holding her there a few seconds longer than normal. I couldn't help it, I loved seeing her this way and feeling her lips against mine.

Especially now that she wasn't *also* kissing Jackson.

"So when's the big day?" her mom asked, pulling me right out of that moment. "Proposal date, not wedding. I know you haven't asked her yet."

Nila touched her lips softly and cleared her throat. "Mom …"

I blushed, trying hard not to appear as taken aback as I was. "Uh … wouldn't that answer ruin the surprise for Nila?"

"Fine, fine. Nila, go away, dear. Go see if Juliet needs you."

She blinked at her mom, then opened her mouth like she was going to argue — then whispered "Sorry" to me and slipped away to leave us alone.

Her mom took my hands in hers. "You've been dating for years. Tell me the truth … did she tell you no? Did she reject you?"

"No, she hasn't. We've been so happy and busy we haven't really had a chance to talk about it. I — did she say something about it? Does she want to get married?" I figured it was as good a moment as any to get some information on her, and maybe I really wanted to deflect.

"All she talks about is you. She may not have mentioned marriage, but I know she wants to. She's just not the type of woman to say it," she explained, patting my hand. "Do you want to marry her or are you just leading her on?"

"Of course I'm not," I rushed out. "I'd never do that to her … I love her." It was the first time I'd ever said it out loud and didn't mean it platonically. "I want to marry her."

I met her mother's eyes to show her I meant it, and the joy I found there only solidified it. "Good. Then take all the time you need. It should be a special thing for both of you, but I can't pretend I wasn't worried. Richard told me your relationship was fake, isn't that ridiculous?"

I flicked my gaze over to Nila's Uncle Richard and frowned. "That's weird. Just because we haven't taken that next step?"

"No. He said it's because he knows unresolved sexual tension when he sees it. I told him he's full of it, but you know how men are," she sighed. "But I also know love when I see it. And you two are going to be fine."

I left the table not sure of how to feel, but after a drink and a refill, I relaxed. Uncle Richard wasn't wrong — I'd never wanted to fuck someone more than I did Nila in my entire life, and that was counting back when I was thirteen and jacking off to a Mrs. Butterworth's syrup bottle at a friend's sleepover.

Puberty was a rough time for everyone, and if my five brothers all told their embarrassing stories, mine wouldn't even be in the top three. Kale might've had us all beat.

I finished another drink and went to walk around the party, smiling when I spotted the DJ and dance floor Nila had said would be there and earning some brownie points by dancing with her grandma.

Nila came over midway through the second song and stole me back, then whispered, "Sorry I left you. What'd she want?"

"Wants to know when I'm going to make an honest woman out of you.

Y'know how parents are. My mom's asked me too." I spun her around and pulled her in, leaning in to steal another kiss.

She blushed after and held me closer. "Guess we're gonna have to come clean eventually, huh? I was hoping we'd be able to wait until one of us got into a legitimate relationship, but she's not wrong. It's been six years, it's weird."

I frowned slightly and stopped dancing, then took her hand and led her to a different room. I didn't respond until we were alone and I saw she was actually nervous. "Is it getting weird for you, Niles?" I asked, concerned.

"No," she said quickly. "Maybe it's weird that it's not weird, but no. I just meant … eventually people are gonna ask too many questions. Like why we aren't having kids or getting married. I thought maybe moving in would help, it's not like two people have to get married or have kids, but … I don't know. Just ignore me."

I reached out for her hand and tugged her in. "I won't ignore my girlfriend …

even if just for tonight." I brushed some hair out of her face and pulled my lip between my teeth. "I say we just ride this train until it ends. Maybe putting a baby in you wouldn't be the worst thing in the world."

"Toby?" she gasped, fisting a hand around my tie. "What are you saying?"

I kissed her before my mouth got me in any more trouble, except kissing my best friend seemed to only dig my grave deeper because once I started, I couldn't fucking stop. We'd kissed before, but *never* like that. I slid my tongue into her mouth and slammed her against the wall, letting my hands slide down lower than ever before so I could grip her ass.

The fucking whimper she let out as she tugged my tie and met that kiss like she'd been dying for it too went straight to my cock, and I felt myself harden against her. My fingers seemed to be doing their own thing; they went even lower, slowly lifting her dress so I could truly slot between those thighs, and when I felt the heat between her legs against my crotch, I moaned. I was right there, only thin fabric blocking me from finally sinking inside Nila's body … but before I could completely give in and rip off her panties, the door opened and I finally snapped out of it.

"Shit!" I backed off her and kept my back to the door, not wanting whoever it was to see my aching hard-on as Nila hastily fixed her dress.

"Oh, gross," Juliet said, making Nila swear quietly and rush forward.

"God, Jules! What are you doing here?"

"I was looking for you two but I didn't expect to see … that."

I looked up and cursed the gods for making this the hardest I'd been in a long time. "Nothing to see here," I said in a strained tone. "Just need a moment to check out the immaculate paint job on the ceiling."

She clicked her tongue as she pulled Nila toward her. "Okay, Casanova. You can get your dick wet later. I need her right now because people showed up that I don't like and I need her to kick some ass."

"Sorry, T." Nila hesitated a moment, then rushed out, "We'll talk tonight, yeah?" as Juliet led her outside.

I took a breath and shook my leg, adjusting myself as I tried to think of a way to get myself to soften. After five useless minutes I caved and pulled out my phone. If anything could help me get rid of a boner, it'd be hearing one of my brothers' voices. I called the first one I saw in my call log and huffed when Brennan's voice filled the other end. "Hey," I said, "what do you do when you have an inappropriate boner at a graduation party and no one to sink into?"

"Um … find someone to sink inside of," he said slowly. "What's going on?"

"Think it's just been too long since I got laid. Swear I'm close to going full Kale and snatching up a cantaloupe. Distract me, how're the kids?"

"No way, I'm not talking about my children when you have a boner. You're at a grad party, you said? Whose?"

"Juliet's. Nila's sister. Her whole family is here so I can't even leave this room until it's gone. Talk about your wife then, how's Nix?"

He sighed quietly. "She's fantastic. You should've led with the fact that Nila gave this boner to you. Explains why you can't just find someone else."

I knew my brother saw right through me, and I wasn't in any place to deny it. "Yeah, kinda stuck. Fuck, it's getting worse, Brennan. I have to fuck her, but if I do, everything could change."

"So what? Let things change. Or tell her that you just need to do it once to get it out of your system. I don't know. My wife would tell you to just communicate. Ask her what she wants and how she feels, then be honest with her."

"Right. You definitely learned that from her. Our family may be known to have big dicks, but we are absolutely not known for being great communicators," I joked, happy to feel that my cock was finally going down.

"So be the one to change that. You two are crazy about each other, any idiot can see it. Just talk to her."

I took a few more moments to breathe before I got off the phone. Knowing everyone around us saw how we felt about each other didn't help.

If they could all see it, why the hell couldn't she?

EIGHT

Fucking Clowns

NILA

I'd waited six years for that kiss. Longer, if I was being technical, but six years at the minimum. The amount of pecks and surface-level smooches we'd shared were too many to count, but a kiss like that? Where I felt like he was seconds away from taking me apart?

That was the first, and I'd been waiting for years.

Being in love with Tobias Novak was the most painful thing I'd ever experienced, because I'd been convinced I was in love alone. But lately, when the other partners dried up and he stopped searching for new ones, when he started touching me more and calling me more and asked me to move in when I needed him … I started to think maybe he loved me too.

And now I knew he did. That kiss wasn't one of lust or boredom, he *needed* me. And with as wet as I was under the damned dress I'd bought solely to impress him, I needed him too. I *ached* for him, which was precisely why I was ready to kill my little sister.

"What could you possibly need me for?" I snapped. I knew I couldn't tell her why I was mad — that she'd interrupted a kiss I'd waited ages for — since I was supposed to be dating the man already, but still. I couldn't believe she did it.

"Pictures, of course. You guys can make out all night if you want, my party is only a few more hours. Did it really get that hot and heavy? Here of all places?"

I wanted to scream, but that would require telling her the truth. It was times like that when I missed Jackie more than anything. She'd have told my sister to shove it for me and steered me right back toward my man, no questions asked. "Yeah, it did. It's fine though, it's not like I don't live with him. But he should be here for pictures, too … and what happened to the people you said you didn't like?"

"It's my best friend's family. They think this party is for her too, and no, this is my day. I don't want them thinking they can be in all the photos." She linked our arms together and tugged me along, pointing out the people she was talking about in a slick manner and then smiling past me. "Your man is coming."

My stomach did an unwelcome somersault as I turned to see Toby walking toward us. I knew his brothers were objectively more good-looking — they were models, after all — but Toby was stunning to me. Gorgeous light brown eyes, square jaw covered in just the right amount of beard, gorgeous eyes, dark hair just long enough to run my fingers through, and muscles for days without being gross about it. He'd had my heart skipping beats from day one, and now that I was getting a taste of how possessive he could be, it was even worse. "Toby," I called, waving him over as I suddenly became a little self-conscious of the way the dress was clinging to my stomach. "You ready for pictures?"

The way his eyes looked me up and down helped that confidence, but I was still nervous as he gripped my hand and smiled down at me. "Picture time already? When's dessert?"

In five minutes if we can ever get out of here, I thought. "Probably after this? Oh, hang on." I leaned past him and hissed to Juliet's friend's parents, "Out! This isn't for you. Shoo."

I could hear Toby struggling not to laugh as they all moved away with offended expressions, but I was just happy they all moved. "Ah, I see why she felt the need to interrupt us."

"Yeah, she needed me to whoop some ass. But we should talk—"

"Okay, everyone! Say cheese!"

I forced a smile as Toby tugged me in by my hip and slapped on that Novak smirk that said they were all born to be in front of a camera, and then he leaned in to whisper in my ear, "Want me to talk? Want me to tell you what I'd be doing to you if your little sister hadn't walked in that room?"

"Fuck," I hissed, clenching my thighs a little and nodding like an idiot. "Yes."

His grip on my hip tightened, and when he leaned in to give me exactly what I wanted, my older sister Ariel screamed out in pain seconds before her water broke.

The whole place was chaos after that, and Toby was by her side in an instant trying to help her sit down. *My siblings fucking hate me,* I thought bitterly, but I'd been waiting so damn impatiently for my nephew to be born that I knew things with Toby could wait.

We made a mad rush to the hospital and Toby stayed behind to help clean up the party. I wished he'd have come with me. I knew our history well enough to know that if we didn't talk about what had happened soon, the moment would pass and we'd never talk about it again — which would put me right back in the awkward, terrible, hellish position of living with a man I wanted to worship without being able to do it.

Still, as Ariel went through labor and I sat in the waiting room with Juliet, my father, and my brother Clay, thoughts of Toby faded. Ariel's partner had dumped her the moment he found out she was pregnant, which meant we'd all be taking bigger roles in the little guy's life than we'd originally thought, and it was time to work out some details.

"We have everything we need," my father said. "She's all moved in and the nursery is ready, but we're going to need more diapers, and maybe formula too if she's unable to breastfeed or chooses not to.

She hasn't made up her mind yet. Will you two go handle that?"

Clay glanced once at me then nodded. "Of course. We'll drop everything off at the house and come back, but call one of us if something happens, okay? I don't like the thought of leaving."

"Your mother is in there with her," he said gently. "She'll be just fine. Now go, the sooner you leave, the sooner you'll get back."

I dragged Clay with me and insisted upon driving, then sped all the way to the store. I had my own selfish reasons for wanting to hurry up that didn't just include my sister and nephew, but Clay thankfully didn't press for details as we raced through the aisles, got what we needed and headed back to the hospital.

Another four hours later, I had a healthy little nephew and a very tired, happy sister, and I was unceremoniously thrown out so she could rest when I overstayed my welcome.

It was just as well … I was exhausted and beyond ready to get out of the heels I'd worn to Juliet's party, and all of me wanted to go kiss Toby until he admitted we were more than friends.

He's a fucking Novak, I reminded myself. *He doesn't do relationships and certainly not with people who give it away for free, so maybe kissing him again isn't the answer. Just talk to him first and see what happens.*

That sounded like a decent enough plan, but when I got home and made my way to his room to see if he was awake, he wasn't even home.

I checked my phone quickly and didn't see a text from him, so I sighed and sent him a gif of a baby then showered and crawled into bed.

So much for that idea.

~

As far as models go, I'd worked with quite a few — but none quite as forward or egotistical as James Shepherd. He was tall, blonde, and built like a god, but he was also an asshole and I had no interest in him.

That didn't stop him from flirting with me as I tried to do his makeup. "Hush," I snapped after a particularly cheesy pickup line. "If you keep running your mouth, I'm going to screw this up."

"Nah, you're a pro. Seriously though, why the hell are you single?" He stayed still after my threat, but his eyes were still locked on me in a way that made me uncomfortable.

"Who says I'm single?" I countered. "Maybe I just don't owe you the details of my personal life." I had half a mind to mess up his makeup just to spite him, but that would hurt Toby in the long run, so I sucked it up and refrained from poking him in the eye.

"You're grouchy today," he said simply, not looking deterred in the slightest. "Guess the Novaks aren't all that in bed, huh?"

"Don't know what the hell that's supposed to mean, but is there a problem here, Nila?" Toby's voice was ice cold as he walked up behind me, nothing like the warm, welcoming man I'd grown to know, and this wasn't the first time I'd heard this tone.

He was ready to fight.

"No problem. I think James here was just trying to ask me out and failing. Isn't that right, James?" I fixed my eyes on him with a half-smirk as he scoffed.

"Yeah, something like that," he admitted, and the flirty smile he flashed me afterward had me softening just a little. "Just wondered what has her in a bad mood, that's all. I miss that smile."

"Probably not in the mood to be harassed at work, James. Do yourself a favor and keep it in your pants until your shoot is done, yeah?" Toby backed away to go talk to Sage, and from the look of his stance, he had every intention of hanging out this entire shoot.

"Okay, you're not the grouchy one. He is. Jeez, it was just a joke … also didn't expect the name drop to summon one."

"It's because you insulted them," I explained, trying not to smile so wide my cheeks hurt. I couldn't help it, I loved it when Toby got jealous. *What's his is his.* "I'm surprised the whole family didn't swoop down on you, honestly. They're very protective of their reputations." I spun him around to fix his hair, then glanced at him in the mirror. "If you ask me, you got off easy."

"Guess I should be grateful it summoned the older, boring one then," he whispered.

Defensiveness rose in my chest. "He's my best friend and he's far from boring."

James huffed a laugh. "Got it. Really though, what's a guy gotta do to get a date with someone as beautiful as you?"

"Nila," Toby interrupted. "Soon as you're done with him, can I talk to you over here?"

The look on his face had me clenching my thighs together as nonchalantly as I could. Part of me wanted to push, to flirt back just to see what Toby did — if he'd punish me, spank me, throw me up against another wall … but I knew how precarious the situation was. I had to be careful. I nodded once to Toby and ignored James completely as I finished up, then wiped my hands off and walked over slowly.

"Everything okay, T?"

"Mmhmm." Toby gently took my hand and led me to a more private corner. "Fucking clown," he muttered. "I was talking to Brennan about changing to the day shift to help out more. Thinking maybe we just carpool most days? What you think?"

I stared down at the birthmark on Toby's wrist as I thought of him being that close so often, and it was as exhilarating as it was terrifying. I'd have no space away from him, no privacy whatsoever. We'd be around each other virtually all day every day … and that would either be amazing or horrific. "Um … yeah," I said after a moment. The flecks of color in his determined eyes had me rooted to the spot as I nodded again to confirm. "Yeah, that would be great. Smart," I added. "Economical and stuff."

"Yeah, it's for economic reasons. We'll use the damn Tesla," he joked, reaching out to touch my hair lightly. "I know it's a lot, but I'll stay out of your way … unless I see asshats harassing you, of course."

I didn't want him to stay out of my way. I wanted him to be *in* my way, all of the time, but I was too much of a chicken to say it right then. "Yeah," I agreed. "Sounds good."

NINE

Maybe We Should Talk

It had been days and things with Nila were still strange. Our easy friendship was still perfectly intact, but it felt like there was something hanging over our heads we needed to talk about. It was just obvious neither of us knew where to begin.

The second I stepped out of my office, I saw Kale walking around with a huge, stupid grin on his face, telling me exactly who he was on the phone with: Zack, the only person in the world to make Kale smile like an asshole.

I whistled to get his attention, then tossed my head toward my door to tell him I needed to see him. He nodded, so I slipped back inside my office and waited for him to come.

"What's up?"

Kale plopped in the chair across from my desk and lifted a foot up to push it back on two legs. He always did that, sat like a child that couldn't sit still and rested his giant weight on two of the four legs… no matter how expensive the chair was. It made me chuckle.

"Stop being weird. Why are you laughing at me?"

"Did you see that meme? The one about how gay people are when sitting?" Kale's feet fell to the ground with a stomp, his unamused gaze answering my question. "It's just funny because of the amount of gay stereotypes you prove wrong on a daily basis, yet not even you could break that one. That gene must be a strong one."

My dramatic brother stood and walked toward the door. "Is this really why you called me in here?"

"No." I approached him with a barely contained smirk. "Just sit down, please. I'll shut up about the meme. I didn't mean to offend you or some shit."

"Not offended… bitch." Kale sat back in the chair, lifting two of its legs off the ground immediately, and then chuckled. "Yeah, fuck off. It's comfortable."

I couldn't help but join in. "I know. I have something under my desk for mine. Sitting straight is overrated."

"Everything straight is overrated. Anyway, can we hurry this up? Zack is at home on his knees for me."

I tried not to cringe at the visual and shook my head. "Poor guy," I quipped, chuckling at yet another unamused expression on his face. "Right, the point. I know I can't really compare our situations because of how you met Zack, but—"

"Love is love. Doesn't matter if Nila kicked your Jeep and you lied about it being yours so you could talk to her, or if you're roommates denying your feelings for each other. You love each other."

If only it were that simple. "We kissed this weekend."

Suddenly, he was very amused. "Fucking finally. Only kissed, though? How'd you get him back in the cage?"

I rolled my eyes. "Not all of us have fucking anacondas in our pants that need to be wrangled in every time they wake." Kale raised an eyebrow at me like he wasn't falling for it and I sighed. "I called Brennan."

"Ah, Of course, Brennan Novak, C.E.O. of Boner-Killing Industries. Anyway, why'd you have to? Did she not want it to go further?"

I thought of how ready she was, how pliant her body was as I went between her legs, the heat radiating onto my cock through the fabric. She wanted it, maybe as much as I did.

My brother's chair fell to the ground. He had a grimace on his face. "Should I go get Brennan? I know that look. Or should I just solve all your problems and call Nila up?"

"Neither. I'm fine. To answer your question, no. She absolutely wanted it to go further. Her sister walked in, it was at her family party."

"And what about when you got home?"

I looked away, because I didn't fucking go home. I was a coward. "Her other sister went into labor and I went to Sage's to … avoid it, I guess. I didn't know what the fuck to do. Then we just didn't talk about it. I'm dying for her, Bror. I don't know what the hell to do."

"I know I'm not the poster child for communication, but when it comes to a lasting relationship, you kind of just have to do it. Zack's always been better at communicating than me and I knew if I wanted to keep him, I'd have to get on board. Start with what you *can* talk about, and then don't hold back as the rest comes to mind. Not talking at all is the worst thing you can do here."

I nodded. It sounded easy enough but there was still one problem for me. "But what's that even mean, start with what I can talk about? I don't know where to begin."

Kale sent off a text before he responded. "I can't say what that means. Maybe start by asking about her sister that had the baby, then maybe the other sister that walked in, then what you were doing when she walked in? Get there naturally and it will flow easier. But honestly, you should just ask her on a date or something. Zack and I fucked the day we met so I don't really know how to navigate it without sex on the table. I always talk easier after a play session and a nut."

"Has anyone ever told you that you over-share?" I deadpanned, making him laugh.

"All the time, actually. Mor says I wasn't born with a filter. Don't mean to change the subject, but is Nila coming to Midsommardagen? Genesis is flying out to come and I think Nila should go. She's family too."

I smiled at that because I was glad my family saw her as one of us and it wasn't just me. "I'll talk to her tonight. About Sweden, specifically. We'll see how that goes before the other stuff."

I said goodbye to my brother and took a seat to think about my approach, but before I could make any decisions, Nila herself walked in. "Hey, how's it going down there?" I asked, trying not to look like I was caught off guard.

"Fine. Just had a break while they reset. Eliza Rose is up next and she hardly needs anything at all," she said, with at least a hint of jealousy. "How are you? I'm not interrupting, am I?"

"Never." I relaxed as I took in her gorgeous features, knowing damn well she had nothing to be jealous of. "Did you give any thought to Sweden? My family is all hoping you'll be there."

"Are they?" She sat down across from me and ran a hand through the ends of her curls. "I got my passport and everything so I don't see why not, but are you sure it's okay? Isn't that usually something that's a big deal for you guys?"

"It's a big deal because it's all about family for us, and you're family. I'm excited to show you my home country even though I was born here. You know my mom, she'd never let us forget where we're from. Genesis is coming by the way, and you know I've been wanting you to meet her. It's her first time going with us all too. You guys can be Sweden noobs together."

She shifted but nodded a little. "Are Kai, Sage or Archie bringing anyone?"

"No. Mor told Arch it's too soon for him to bring his new girlfriend and Sage and Kai are single and none of their friends can come. Does that make you nervous or something?" I could tell it did, I just couldn't understand why. She'd been to enough of my family parties to not be.

"Not at all. I just thought maybe we should talk before the trip? About what happened at Juliet's party?"

And there it was. "Yeah, we probably should." I grabbed an Eldan International pen off my desk and started fidgeting with it, letting my brain wander slightly at how we should really change that name someday. "Here, or like at home?"

"Here, maybe? You know how we are. It's already been a couple of weeks." She cleared her throat and leaned forward. "Were you just horny?"

"No," I said honestly. "I was horny obviously, but not for just anyone." It was my turn to squirm in my seat. "I'd wanted to kiss you for a long time, not just the pecks we do to put on a show, legitimately kiss you, and once I started I couldn't stop. I didn't want to stop even if I *did* want to. Fuck, is this coming out wrong?"

"If you meant to make no sense, then no, it's coming out just fine. You wanted to stop?"

There was nothing on her face to guide me here — nothing in those eyes to tell me whether she wanted me to say yes or no, so I went with the truth.

"No. I didn't want to stop, Nila. Did you?" *Give me something here, sweetheart.*

She stared at me in silence for an agonizingly long moment, then shook her head slightly. "No, T. I didn't want to stop."

I took a calm breath as the world righted itself on its axis. I wasn't alone, Archie and everyone else weren't wrong, because she wanted me too. I stood up and walked around my desk, reaching out a hand for hers and pulling her to stand. "That's all I needed to hear." I kissed her before she could respond, then lifted her up on the desk so I could take my place between her thighs and grind myself against her. She melted into me, moaning into my mouth like she'd been dying for it just as much as I had, and I didn't give a shit where we were anymore. I needed her. "How much longer is your break, sweetheart?"

I kissed down her neck as she moaned my name and wrapped her legs around me. "Not long … fuck, T! The shoot is in ten minutes, I only have like five," she rushed out, reaching down to work on my belt. "Is that long enough?"

"Fuck no," I growled, pulling back so I could work on her jeans, and when she lifted her ass for me I could feel my hands trembling. I'd been with plenty of women in my life, and yet I was as nervous as I had been my very first time. "My cock will just have to wait, but your pussy won't." I spread her legs, ignoring the throbbing between mine, and stared down at her panties as I leaned in and inhaled her scent. It was purely her, mixed with some scented lotion I couldn't pinpoint, but it was one she'd used for years. I'd always loved it, but here where I could smell her delicious pussy, I was sure it was the best scent in the world. I slid off those panties for another sniff, then pocketed them as I reached to slide two fingers inside of her. "Smell so fucking good, Niles."

"Jesus Christ, T." The look on her face was all innocence and need — wide eyes, pinched brows, lips parted beautifully as she leaned back a little further to give me better access. "Oh, fuck …"

I couldn't wait to taste her any longer. I dropped down before she could even process what I was doing and sucked in her clit, my fingers curling inside her as I growled.

She rocked those thick, beautiful hips up and twitched as I moved just right, so I held there and took her apart until she was dripping all over my desk and clamping a hand over her own mouth to stifle her moans.

It was everything I'd dreamed of and more, and I suddenly imagined living and dying right there between her thighs. I needed this every fucking day, and I was man enough to beg for it if I had to. I curled my fingers again, so hard in my slacks I could've ripped them … and then she came.

The way her thighs shook and her breath caught in her lungs had me digging my nails into her hips and groaning so loud I was sure people heard. I slowed as she came down, lapping with every twitch of her body, and when she exhaled I sat up to show her the mess she'd made.

"Toby … I—" Her phone rang, interrupting her and making her cuss. "It's Sage. Just stay here, okay? Don't let anyone else in. I'll be back as soon as I can." She pulled me in to lick the taste of herself off my lips, then pulled her jeans up and shuddered when the fabric touched her skin. "Make sure there's room for me under your desk when I come back."

I watched her leave and pressed down on my aching cock, then pulled her panties out of my pocket to smell them again. It didn't help with my boner, but it did help calm me enough to move back to my seat and wait for her. It was excruciating, and it took everything I had not to call Sage and tell him to fuck off.

Why did a sibling always have to ruin it?

It took twenty minutes for her to slip back through the door, but she didn't say a word as she locked it behind her and came over to slide underneath my desk. She was silent as she licked her lips and locked eyes with me, silent as she finished undoing my belt, and silent as she swallowed me fucking whole.

I, on the other hand, was the opposite. I moaned her name so pathetically I should have been embarrassed, but she looked so fucking good with my cock in her throat that I couldn't seem to care. "You're so fucking beautiful."

She gagged just enough to get me wet, then pulled off to stroke. "Remember that porn I sent you? Did you picture me?" she asked, sucking me back in and stroking the base so perfectly that I could barely think straight.

"Fuck yeah I did," I groaned, slotting my fingers into her hair as I thrusted up. "Pictured you choking on my cock just like this. Wanted to eat your pussy on my desk for years."

The pleased noise she released had me losing myself to her mouth, and within minutes, I was done. I came hard, twitching as my cock pulsed in my best friend's mouth, and when she pulled off to show me the results on her tongue, I thought I was going to die.

Yeah, she is definitely the one for me.

TEN

Midsommardagen

I'd missed the last two family trips to Sweden because of work, so landing in the place of my ancestors felt amazing. I knew some of my brothers didn't take our Viking heritage seriously, but most of us did — and Sage showing up with his long hair and beard all in braids just proved it to me.

Since we had so many people with us who didn't speak Swedish, we kept it to a minimum as we made our way to our landställe. The summer house looked exactly as I remembered — huge, square and white with black shutters, nestled back in the woods with a private lake behind it. It wasn't our family's only residence in Sweden, but it was the only one large enough to accommodate all fourteen of us.

As much as I wanted to share a room with Nila, my mother put her with Genesis to help her acclimate a little better and stuck me with Archie. As roommates went, Archie was the favorable choice. He wasn't loud or messy, and he was such a romantic that I knew he'd help me sneak around to see Nila if I asked him to.

That would have to wait though, as would the actual Midsummer celebrations, which wouldn't officially kick off until tomorrow. For now, we were grilling out by the lake to relax after that ridiculously long flight.

I watched as Nila got a drink for Genesis and slowly started swaying as Kai began playing the guitar, and the second he started singing everyone around us went silent. There was something about Kai's voice that could make anyone need to stop what they were doing and simply listen. It was a voice that would bring out unbidden emotions you didn't realize were bubbling under the surface and make you gravitate toward the one you loved. All my siblings had some sort of talent, and to be fair most of my brothers sang really well; we just couldn't compare to Kairo.

When Nila sat next to me I bumped her gently with my shoulder, smiling at her as she leaned a little closer.

"I'll never get tired of listening to him," she said softly. "Or seeing how at peace he looks when he plays. Like all the things that weigh him down just … vanish."

"I think for a little while, they do. I mean, I feel lighter just listening to him. I think he should put out an album but I don't think he wants to."

I looked around at my family and noticed how tightly my mother was holding my nephews. I wondered if she got any release while Kai sang too. She looked much heavier than she used to, even with all the weight loss, and I couldn't stop the anger at my father that rose in my chest once again.

Nila seemed to sense the shift in my mood and squeezed my thigh with her hand. "Breathe, T. It's a beautiful night and we're in a beautiful place. And tomorrow you get to watch me dance around a pole with flowers in my hair."

"I get to, huh?" My attention was firmly back on her. "So you promise more beautifulness tomorrow? Is that what you're saying? Only that beauty will make my dick hard." I whispered the last part, but the fact that we still hadn't fucked was bothering me. Oral was one thing, but I wanted it all.

"Maybe we should've stayed in a hotel," she whispered back, glancing up at me through her eyelashes. "Do they even know about us?"

I shook my head. "Not yet, haven't really had a chance to say anything. Mor will be ecstatic, but I wasn't sure how to say it. She was so focused on this trip I didn't want to interrupt and I don't know. Should I just kiss you and let them all see?"

"So sure of yourself all the time, and such a mess when it comes to me," she teased. "You don't have to tell them if you're not ready. I know that's a big thing for you guys, especially here."

I nodded, not wanting her to think I was unsure of her. "I was thinking maybe at family dinner back home."

Kai stopped singing then so he could get a drink, and the chatter around us picked up again. Kale was on drink number five and clinging to Zack like he might float away, and Brennan was only marginally better with Phoenix, but my other brothers were normal enough to stay around the fire and ask Genesis how she'd been.

Nila got up pretty quickly after I told her I wouldn't be telling anyone until we got home, but she didn't seem angry. It was more like she knew we needed distance if we wanted to keep things under wraps, and that included when we said goodnight. All I got was a hug and a kiss on the cheek before she followed Gen into their room, and I spent the whole damn evening dodging Archie's questions about her until we both passed out.

The next morning, breakfast was insane with fourteen people. I barely saw her at all until we were loading up to head to the local park to start the festivities, and even then, she ended up in a different car than I did. Brennan kept looking at me like he thought I was going to explode, and maybe I was — the dress Nila was wearing had my brain on one, single track … and it had nothing to do with the decorated maypole that had been erected in the center of the park. I had to deal with Genesis texting me questions about Nila while we drove, and I got her to reluctantly back off when I promised to call her if anything big happened between us.

Nila finally approached me when everyone else started dancing and nodded toward the maypole. "So I've heard of these, but I have no idea what the hell it is. What's the deal?"

"Depends on who you ask," I explained. "Some think it started as a symbol of fertility. That's supposedly how Midsummer started — it was an ancient fertility festival since we thought the solstice was a good time to conceive. But Mor's the only one of us that really believes that. Most of us believe the other legend: that the pole has roots in Norse mythology and represents a link between the underworld, earth and heavens. See, the solstice is said to be a time of year when magic is strongest. Ripe for rituals and predictions, stuff like that. Some people pick bouquets of seven flowers and put them under their pillow."

"Okay, I have to ask. Why?" she asked.

"To dream of their future partner. Who knows if it works or not, but I wouldn't knock anything that deals with the gods."

Nila eyed the maypole with new respect and gently touched the flower crown in her hair. "Huh. Maybe I'll have to try that."

"Maybe you do," I leaned in to whisper, stealing a quick kiss to her cheek when I thought no one was watching, but of course I was wrong. Archie saw, and the smile he wore made me want to slap him. "Pole then flowers?"

She only thought about it for a moment before taking my hand and dragging me toward the people dancing, and her laughter overrode any embarrassment as we joined in with everyone else.

I wasn't the only one who noticed how beautiful she was in the blue and white sundress she'd chosen, but I also knew I was the only one that was allowed to touch her, and that made me just a little grabbier than I meant to be. "Tell me I can see you tonight after bedtime."

"Mmm … maybe." She pinched her tongue between her teeth and twirled again, then reached out to pull me in by my shirt. "Gen's much better at braiding hair than you, so I don't know."

My grip on her hip tightened. "I can guarantee I'm better at other things than her, do you need a reminder?"

She gasped quietly and nodded, melting into me a little then pulling back. "There are people watching. See that little store to our left and the alley next to it? Think we could sneak away?"

"I'll go first and check it out, follow me in five." I slipped away and ensured the alleyway was empty and then fully regretted saying five minutes. All that did was give me plenty of time to pace.

When she finally appeared, I wasted no time pushing her against the wall and catching her in a consuming kiss, one she opened easily for. I felt her hands in my hair and her tongue in my mouth as every inch of her pressed up against me, and I couldn't understand how we'd made it so long without doing this.

"T," she gasped out, kissing me again and again as my hands roamed her body and lifted her dress. "Touch me."

I was inches away from touching that sweet pussy, I just needed to taste her again — but before I could, I heard Kale chuckle behind us. "Fuck," I whispered and pulled away. I gave him the dirtiest look I could muster for interrupting, but seeing Zack under his arm made me lose some of my anger. "Really?"

He set his husband down without any shame and a face filled with amusement. "Didn't know the alleyway was occupied. Come on, Pojke. We have to wait our turn."

They walked away, but Nila was staring after them like she'd never seen them before. "What does that mean? 'Pojke?'"

I snorted. "It's not as cute as it sounds. It means 'boy.' He calls him 'boy' and Zack fucking loves it."

Her eyes widened a little. "That's kinda hot."

I smirked, moving back in closer to cage her against the wall. "Is it, Rövhål?"

"If that means 'girl,' it's still hot," she breathed, reaching down to palm me. "Nice try."

"It doesn't actually." I kissed along her neck toward her ear and rutted into her hand as I whispered, "It means asshole."

She gasped loudly and shoved me back with a wide, shocked smile, then flipped her hair over her shoulder with all the attitude I'd come to expect from her. "Rude. Hope your balls hurt now."

"Fuck. Yeah, they do." I watched her ass move side to side as she walked away, like I was being hypnotized by it, and suddenly regretted being a jackass. I knew she wasn't upset with me, but I also knew I'd missed out on getting even the tiniest bit of release, so I decided to blame the person truly responsible … Kale.

Him and Zack were nowhere to be found of course, and by the time they turned up again, my anger had dissipated into mild annoyance and I made my way over. "Hey, Pojke," I said mockingly, but based on Kale's face he had gotten plenty of release because he didn't look offended in the slightest.

"What? We gave you some privacy." He kissed Zack's head and walked away, and I could tell Zack felt bad for cockblocking as he awkwardly tugged on his collar.

"You having a good time, Zack? You look a little tense."

"Oh. Yeah, I'm good," he said, and I didn't miss the hoarseness in his voice that I didn't want to ask about. "Do you know how long this lasts though? Kale wouldn't tell me and I have … reasons for wanting it to be over soon," he whispered. "Kinda dying over here."

"You and me both, Bror." Zack may not have been my brother by blood, but I loved him for Kale, and none of us could have hand-picked someone better for him if our lives depended on it. "Only lasts like three days, we're fine right?"

The slight smile on his face faded quickly. "Oh, fuck. Yeah … totally fine. I gotta go, but you two make a really cute couple. I'm happy for you." He waved and pivoted to run after Kale, and I couldn't help but laugh as I watched him tug on his husband's arm and give him puppy dog eyes.

I turned my attention back to where Nila was dancing with Genesis and watched her in awe. He wasn't wrong, we did make a cute couple — but I knew the cute part was all her. The next step was getting off my ass and making it official … I just had to figure out how.

ELEVEN

Spanking Included

Sweden was everything my family needed and more. I still hadn't actually slept with Nila, but sneaking around was more fun than I'd expected it to be. We were a couple of high schoolers all over again, and although I loved every second of it, I was ready to fuck my best friend.

Beyond ready.

But when we woke up that first morning back home, something felt off. "Morning," I said as I walked into the kitchen. My greeting earned nothing more than a polite smile before she turned back toward the stove. "You sleep okay?"

"Yeah, of course. Did you?" she asked, aggressively flipping the pancakes she was making. "Felt good to be back in my bed again."

"Yeah." I watched her curiously for a moment before grabbing some coffee. "You got plans today?"

She nodded a little and licked her lips slowly as she turned. "Yeah, I have to go help Clay paint his basement. He just fixed it up; he's turning it into some kind of man cave."

"Oh, that's awesome. Need any help?"

"Really?" She eyed me suspiciously. "You're offering to come help us paint?"

"If you or Clay needed help, yeah. Labor isn't that outside the norm for me, don't sound so surprised. Mor always made us do shit like that because she said there were enough of us to figure it out."

Nila laughed, then set a plate in front of me. "Sorry, I wasn't trying to insinuate you weren't capable. I just know it's boring, that's all. I'd love the help and I'm sure he would, too."

I felt better, because all of me was convinced she'd say no, convinced that she needed a break from me or something. I was happy to be wrong. "Alright, I'll drive. I helped Kale with his … cave. I don't know what to call it, we'll just call it a basement. Clay's should be a piece of cake unless he's also going for the whole sex dungeon feel."

She snorted, covering her mouth to try to hide it. "No, and I'd like to think he'd ask someone more qualified for help if he was."

"Hey! I've got one sex dungeon under my belt. I got this," I joked, just happy to see her smile. "Did you have a good time in Sweden?" *Because I did and it felt so right with you there, but I'm too much of a coward to tell you that.*

"It was better than I imagined," she admitted, blushing faintly. "I didn't understand half the things you guys said to each other, but it was really cool to be included in that. Thanks for inviting me."

"I told you, you're family, and honestly I don't think we even noticed we were talking in Swedish most of the time. I really tried not to. You should learn it, Kale is teaching Zack in some weird roleplay game — yeah, he fucking overshares — but we can start doing little lessons together … minus the spankings." *Unless you're into that too.*

That blush deepened, but she smiled playfully. "Way to suck all the fun out of it, T. You wouldn't believe the way my ass bounces."

"Nila," I growled, the handle on my porcelain cup snapping off in my grip. "Fucking Hel. Is that an invitation?"

Her breathing picked up as she stared at the cup. "Are you gonna be rough like that?"

I looked down at what I'd done and huffed, surprisingly not embarrassed in the slightest. "Can't really help that part, Niles."

"Then yes, it's an invitation. I don't even care if you teach me Swedish or not," she whispered breathlessly. "God, you make me so fucking wet."

I was on my feet in seconds, spinning her around and bending her over the counter before I could attempt to stop myself. "You tell me this now … when we have somewhere to be." I rubbed circles on her ass, the blood rushing down to my cock so quickly my vision blurred. "When I can't take my time with you." I slapped hard once, groaning at the bounce under my hand, then summoned all the strength I could from the Allfather and backed away. "Going to fuck the hell out of you one day, Niles. I'll tie up every interrupting sibling we have if that's what it'll take."

"I'd rather you tied me up, but whatever you have to do." She stood fully and turned toward me, pupils blown. "We could tell him we'll handle it and play while we're there," she offered. "He's been dying to go get his furniture but told himself he wouldn't until the paint was done."

"Yeah?" I moved her hair out of her face and kissed her forehead. "What kind of playing do you have in mind?" I knew it would kill me, but I slid my fingers into her pajamas and rubbed her clit, making her twitch and moan my name like a prayer.

"I have one of those w-wearable vibrators," she mumbled. "There's an app."

I stopped moving completely but still applied pressure. "You're so fucking hot, sweetheart. Feel what you do to me?" I pressed my hard cock against her, sighing involuntarily when she palmed me.

"Uh huh, I feel you, baby. I'm yours today … however you want to play. Spanking included." She carefully pulled my hand away and stepped around me. "Eat your breakfast and get dressed. We're going to be late."

I sniffed my fingers in front of her with a smirk, then sucked them into my mouth. "Breakfast was delicious but I need more. Good thing I'm the most patient Novak there is."

"Thought that was Archie," she quipped, but she was gone before I could admit she was right.

An hour later, we were alone in Clay's basement surrounded by cans of burgundy paint, two lawn chairs, a couple of blankets and more plastic than I'd seen in a long time. She'd been brilliant convincing him to leave, and so gorgeously shy as she downloaded the app for me on my phone that I didn't know what to do with her … except give her exactly what she asked for.

"The controls are there." She pointed to my screen. "This side changes the pattern and this side changes the intensity. Pull the slider all the way down to turn it off."

"Got it." I smiled, leaning in for one soft kiss before turning away to grab a roll brush. "To be safe we need to keep it down, okay? That means one spanking for every moan, and no coming until I give you permission. Let's do this."

"Yes, Tobias." She bent over right in front of me to grab a roller of her own, then got to work — but I kept that vibrator inside of her off as I started painting the left wall.

I could see her glancing at me every few seconds, confusion and curiosity lining her features, and I tortured her the best way I could think of: with nothing. I was halfway through one of the longest walls before I pulled my phone out at all, and even then, I watched her clench in my periphery as she prepared for the vibration.

Only … I didn't do it. I was dying to, even hovered my finger over the button, but I didn't want her to expect it. I wanted to catch her off guard and I could tell she was getting frustrated. When I finally gave her what she craved, I didn't pull my phone out at all — I slid my hand into my sweats pocket and pressed it, my cock twitching when she released a surprised moan.

I set the brush down with a grin and slowly made my way over to her, breathing down her neck as I rubbed her perfectly plump ass and prepared her for her first spank. "What was that, baby?"

"God, I'm so fucking wet I could die. I'm sorry, Tobias." She turned her face to meet my eyes and didn't look sorry at all — she looked like she'd been waiting for me to punish her for years.

I pulled back to slap hard, pressing myself against her immediately so I could kiss her neck and then I pressed the button again. "Breathe."

It was broken and shallow, but she sucked in a breath and let her eyes flutter closed as we listened to the vibrator tease her. I could feel her tense, feel her body shift as she pressed those beautiful, voluptuous thighs together, and the way she tucked her bottom lip between her teeth and whimpered had me dying for her.

"You're absolutely perfect, Niles. Perfect and all mine." It took everything to back away and go back to work, but I continued to tease her every few moments.

By the time the first wall was done I was permanently hard, my hand sore from all the random spankings. I couldn't concentrate enough to start the second wall, so instead, I pulled one of the lawn chairs over and sat right behind her with my phone in my hand. Over and over, I changed the patterns and speeds, never letting her get used to anything. I watched her hand shake as she tried to paint, watched her thighs clench and her ass stretch out her shorts when she bent to get more paint, and I watched as she dropped to her knees with the roller pressed to the wall when she'd finally had enough.

"Toby please," she whispered when she saw me looking. "Please let me come."

There was no world where I could deny her. I was on my feet in seconds and rushing over to cradle her face. "Breathe, sweetheart. I got you. You're going to come with my cock in your mouth, okay? Take it out."

"Yes, Tobias." She hastily yanked my sweats down and licked all over my aching cock until I was grabbing her ponytail and guiding her on, and she swallowed me whole as I turned up the intensity on her vibe.

It was fucking heaven, seeing and feeling her fall apart on my cock as her moans sent delicious vibrations straight to my balls. "Fuck, Nila. Most beautiful woman in the fucking world, you know that? Come for me, let me feel that throat squeeze my cock."

Her nails dug into my hips as she flexed her throat and sucked hard, and I could see it in her eyes when she came all over that toy inside of her. I'd never been so jealous of an inanimate object before, feeling her clench and squeeze and gush all around it, and I couldn't stop myself from snapping my hips and pinning her face to my pelvis. "Nila!" I growled, pulling back just once to try and find a rhythm, but it felt so fucking good I failed. I came so deep in her throat she wouldn't taste it at all, and then I slowly moved in and out as we caught our breath. "So fucking hooked on you and I haven't even had your pussy. Can't wait to fill every single hole with my come."

She jerked, moaning low and closing her eyes as I held her there, and she had tears on her cheeks and a mix of drool and saliva dripping down her chin as I let her up. That toy was still pulsing and making her shake, and she cupped her pussy as she looked up to meet my eyes. "T—" she hiccupped a breath, reaching up to pull me down to her. "Please."

I kissed her, turning off the vibrator so she could breathe, but I could tell she needed more. And so did I.

"Touch me. Please, I need your fingers." She grabbed my shirt and kissed me deeply, spreading her legs. I slid one arm around her and the other hand inside her shorts to pull the vibe out of my way. She was so fucking wet my vision went blurry, and I bit along her jaw as I fingered her like it was the last thing I'd ever do. "Love how you can take all of me, sweetheart. Already dying for your taste. You gonna give me something to lick clean?"

"Oh, fuck," she hissed, rocking on my hand and fisting my shirt. "Yes … fuck yes!"

"Not yet, I want to hear your pussy suck my fingers a little longer. Sounds so good, Nila." I closed my eyes and cursed in Swedish under my breath, listening to her dripping pussy as my cock searched for more. "Let me hear you say please."

"Please," she moaned, gasping for air and riding my fingers faster. "Please, T!"

I grunted involuntarily and then curled my fingers. "Come for me, Nila. Better hurry unless you want your brother to come home and see you all strung out like this," I whispered quickly, leaning in to hold her tighter and bite her earlobe. "How do you think he'd feel seeing his baby sister so eager to be stuffed full, so ready to come apart for me?"

She screamed my name as she soaked my fingers, my palm, and the shorts she was wearing as she came, and I took my time licking my fingers clean as she gained control of herself again.

"Come on," I said when I was done. "We still have to finish painting."

TWELVE

What's His is His

MILA

What's his is his.

I was slack-jawed as I watched Toby peel off the tight t-shirt he'd soaked while washing his car, and realized with a jolt that this was how I'd made him feel. All those erections he'd failed to hide, the way his eyes would rake down my frame like he really believed he'd devour me whole if I let him … and I *would* let him, so why hadn't he?

That burning, incessant question was at the forefront of my mind as I called Ariel and told her I was stopping by to see her and the baby. Our parents were out of town for a business conference and I knew she was overwhelmed and exhausted. Besides, if I were being honest with myself, I was looking for any excuse to get away from Toby for a couple of hours and just breathe until I figured out what the hell was going on.

We'd been doing so well … Sweden had been phenomenal and hot, all those times he'd caged me against a wall or a counter when we got back home lived in my head rent-free, and I knew I'd remember that scene in my brother's basement until I died, but we couldn't seem to take that last step.

"I'm leaving," I called to him. "Be back soon."

He waved as he dried off and I slipped out to my car, then warred with myself on the ride to Ariel's. It was awful not being able to talk to my big sister about this — she, like the rest of my family, thought we'd been dating for years — which meant

I was going to have to get my shit together before we arrived so she wouldn't be suspicious.

Or … I could just come clean.

Yeah, that'll go over well. Families just love it when you lie to them.

My parents' house was bigger than they needed — not as egregiously huge as most of the Novaks' houses, but big enough to make me roll my eyes a little as I pulled into the driveway. For Ariel's sake, I was glad they had the extra room for her and my nephew, but I knew my mom was already having a hard time keeping up with the place. At three stories tall and wider than two regular-sized houses, I felt like I had to walk a mile just to climb the concrete steps to the enclosed sunroom that served as a front porch, and every step just made me more nervous to go inside.

She's going to see right through me. She always sees right through me.

Those fears were at least pushed aside as I walked in and heard Phillip crying. Ariel was crying too, and when I rounded the corner to the living room and saw her trying to rock him to calm him down, I noticed how tired she really was. The house around her was a disaster of shocking proportions — there were dirty burp rags strewn everywhere, footie pajamas with the legs inside out draped over the side of the Pack 'n Play, and at least four half-empty bottles laying around.

My heart broke for her.

"Ariel, you should've called me!" I hissed, kneeling in front of her and holding out my arms. The smell of her hit me like a freight train and I nearly gagged, but fuck, she was doing this all by herself. I couldn't have been more impressed or proud of her for still being awake and alive at all. "Go. Get some food, take a hot shower, and take a nap. I've got him, okay? I'm not going anywhere."

She nodded like a zombie and cried harder, so I snapped my fingers to pull her back to reality and sent her on her way. I listened to her rummage around in the kitchen to eat and then craned my neck to hear the shower running a few minutes later. Only then did I look around the house and get to work. Ariel was good, and now it was time to deal with all of … that.

There were instructions for mixing the formula on the fridge with an eating schedule next to it, so I set an alarm on my phone, changed Phillip's diaper, got him dressed, and laid him in the adorable, animal-themed electronic swing that my Aunt Monica had gotten him. Once he was settled, I shot a quick text to Toby to let him know I'd be gone a lot longer than I thought and sent a picture of the mess in the living room before getting started cleaning it.

It took me the better part of two hours to get everything done — it might not have been so bad, but Phillip didn't want to stay in the swing. He wanted to be held, to be paced around in a circle while I sang what were arguably inappropriate songs for an infant, and he wanted food before my alarm went off. I had a brand-new appreciation for exactly how hard having a baby would be full-time, especially alone, and made a mental note to go get an IUD instead of the birth control shots I'd been on.

I wasn't exactly convinced I ever wanted one of my own.

By the time everything was done and Phillip was finally asleep, I was ready for a nap myself. The little guy was swaddled tight in my arms but I was afraid that if I moved a muscle, he'd wake up, so I didn't even reach for the remote to entertain myself. Instead, I let my mind wander.

To Jackie, and how much I missed her, how I hoped that wherever she ended up, she was happy. To how badly my chest ached when I thought of her and the void she'd left in my life. I changed tactics quickly and thought back to those days in high school when the Novaks seemed unreal just to distract myself – they'd been devilishly handsome, athletic, great musicians, and absolute cads — they hadn't seemed like they belonged in a world full of regular people. Now, years later, even though I knew most of them well enough to hang out alone if the desire ever came up, I still felt that way. They *weren't* normal people. Knowing them was special and I'd known that even then … back when I was still so uncomfortable with my thick, dimpled thighs that made it impossible to find jeans, and my stomach rolls that made everything seem either too tight or too baggy, to think someone like him would give me the time of day.

Now, I knew I was beautiful. I couldn't have cared less if anyone else knew that or not — I was comfortable with who I was, I'd learned how to shop for my body type, and I was proud when I looked in the mirror and saw myself standing tall. Right around the time that change had happened, I'd reconnected with Toby and thought maybe, just maybe it was time to make a move … and then he'd never asked for a second date. We'd fallen into the greatest friendship I'd ever heard of, let alone been a part of, and that was that.

Until now.

"How is he?"

Ariel's voice made me jump slightly as I shifted and tried to push the thoughts of Toby away. "He's asleep," I whispered. "Did you nap?"

"Yeah, for about three hours. I can't tell you how much I needed that. Bring him upstairs, we'll put him down in his crib."

She helped me stand without jostling him too much, and we put him to bed and stood side-by-side over his crib as he blew a little raspberry in his sleep. "He's gorgeous, Ariel," I said quietly. "You did so good, Mamma."

"Yeah, I know," she said proudly, reaching in to adjust his blanket. "I don't want to leave him alone while he's swaddled, but I don't think he'll wake up if we stay quiet. Sit with me."

We settled on the grey loveseat on the other side of the room, and we couldn't have been sitting for more than thirty seconds before she sighed dramatically and patted my knee. "Spill."

"Huh?" I did my best to look innocent and confused, but one raised eyebrow from her had me deflating. "I need to tell you something, but I don't know how to say it."

"In English would be best," she said pointedly. "I know something's bothering you, and now that I feel like a person again, I want to know what."

I took a deep breath and decided to just say it simply. "I'm not really dating Toby. I never have been. I got tired of everyone always grilling me because I wasn't ready to settle down, so he offered to help."

"What?" Ariel's eyes widened and she blinked slowly, like one of those times she'd open her eyes again and I'd tell her I was kidding. "I've seen you two. I've seen you kiss and hold hands and touch, even when you didn't think anyone else was looking. The hell do you mean you've been lying about it?"

"That's just it, Ariel. We never did any of that stuff unless we were around the family. It always seemed like those days were different, like *we* were different."

She hummed, then leaned back and crossed her arms as her eyes darted toward her son. "And you're telling me this now because …?"

"Because I *am* actually in love with him, and because we *did* kiss when no one else was around. We did a little more than that, but I'll spare you the details and just say we haven't had sex yet," I admitted. "I don't know why."

My sister shook her head in disbelief. "Don't you? If you can't think of a single reason why not, the problem has to be with him, and I don't believe that. The only reason any of us bought your little lie was because he seemed so … *taken* with you. Like he'd torch anyone that ever got in your way and drown anyone who touched you. In my experience, legitimate guy best friends are protective and amazing, but not to that level. You have to really love someone for that."

What's his is his.

"I guess it's me," I mumbled, staring down at my socks as I wiggled my toes. "I'm afraid."

"Afraid of what?"

"That right now, we can go back," I explained. "We messed around and kissed and touched, but we've always been at least sort of physical with each other. I could chalk it up to curiosity and loneliness and go back to believing I'd be a groomswoman at his wedding, not his bride. If we take that last step, if I *know* how it feels to have him consuming me … I don't think I'd ever be able to go back. He's a Novak, Ariel. I guess I'm still just a little intimidated by all of it."

She thought about that for a moment. "Are you intimidated because you don't want to risk your friendship, or because you don't think you could hold his attention if it becomes more?"

There it was. The real question, the whole reason I'd chosen to tell her the truth. I'd wondered that myself a thousand times, but I knew I'd never come up with the answer until I heard it from someone else. "The first. Toby doesn't even hook up anymore, all he wants to do is spend time with me even when we're not doing anything sexual. I know I could hold his attention. But I can't live without him."

"Well … you can. Whether you like it or not, your world would keep spinning if he wasn't in it anymore. You lived without him once, you could do it again if it ever came to that. But I guess the real question is … can you see yourself with anyone else and still keeping Toby around?"

I thought of all the dates I'd been on and the way they'd all bolted for the hills. I thought of Jackson, and how I told Toby that I'd been the one to call it off, but I wasn't. He'd dumped me when I couldn't tell him I'd move out of Toby's place if things between us got serious. Jackson had every right to end things, especially since I was effectively cheating on him even though it wasn't quite that simple, but I'd known Toby would take it badly and I couldn't bear the thought of him changing the way he acted around me simply so the next guy wouldn't run.

"No," I said honestly. "No, I can't."

"Then I think you know what you need to do. Just don't rush into it, okay? Let it happen naturally, but don't stop yourself from going for it when it does."

She was right and I knew it. I didn't want other people, I wanted him. I wanted the dirty talking and the possession and the bossiness and the spanking and the way he lit me on fire from the inside out. No one else would ever be enough, and I could never go back.

I needed him too badly to go back.

What's his is his … and maybe I just need to get over myself and let him have it.

THIRTEEN

Permission Granted

Nila was called in first thing in the morning and was gone well before I ever got out of bed. I got through an entire breakfast and an episode of *Prison Break* before I heard from her, and when she called, I couldn't fight the grin. "Morning, beautiful. Coming home yet?"

"Um … not exactly," she said carefully. "Sage needs my help with a shoot later."

I groaned. "Of course he does. Tell him to fuck off."

"I don't want to. E.I. landed the Spokane Footwear contract, and he wants to do the shoot outside since the slogan is something about being tough enough to weather any storm, and I think it's going to be awesome. I haven't been invited to any of his crazy shoots before."

She sounded so excited that I nearly went fully Supportive Toby on her, but one press of my remote toward the news had me backtracking entirely. "He wants to do the photoshoot in the storm of course, but this isn't just some storm, Niles. There are fucking tornado watches."

"They can't possibly know what will happen yet," she argued. "Just because it's a storm capable of producing tornadoes doesn't mean it will, and we'll be safe, T. Sage has a basement we can go in if things get crazy. He wants to do it in that field behind his house."

"It's not worth the risk, beautiful. Just come home," I pleaded. My brother liked to push his luck sometimes and I was absolutely going to yell at his ass after, but I needed to get through to her first.

It was a mark of how well I knew her that I knew she was pouting when she went silent. "Or I go, it's exhilarating and crazy and I come home with my adrenaline pumping and ride you on our kitchen floor. Sounds worth the risk to me."

"Fuck," I whispered sharply, unable to deny it went straight to my cock. "Just for science, if I were to say, 'No. you can't go,' you'd respond with …?"

"Telling you that you being all protective and controlling makes me wet, but I'm gonna go anyway, T. I'm sorry. Don't you think Sage will keep me safe?"

"I think Sage will keep everyone safe, but if it's Eliza going, she'd be his priority. You need to be *someone's* first priority, so that settles it, I'm coming and you'll be mine."

Nila let out a tiny little gasp, and I knew I had her. "Yeah, okay. Yep. That works. The office is on the way, do you want to just pick me up?"

"Yeah, I'll put pants on. I was waiting for you in my boxers by the way, I had every intention of taking you the second you walked through that door." I smirked when I heard her fight a moan, then turned off the TV to go dress.

"Can't do that shit to me, T. See you soon."

She hung up, and I instantly called my infuriating younger brother.

"Tobias! If you're calling to yell at me, I'm gonna hang up and you can try again and leave it on a voicemail."

"Then I won't yell," I said through gritted teeth. "I'll gently remind you that the news just mentioned being on a tornado watch, and tell you that Nila isn't going."

Sage scoffed. "I'll return her home to you safely, man. How does she feel about you making decisions for her? Being her work-boss, her roommate, and her best friend isn't enough?"

No, no it's not. Not even close. "Fuck off. The roommate part is still kind of new, and she's too excited to back out on her own so now I'm telling you instead. Get someone else. Why her? We have like twenty makeup artists just here in Whitecrest since Brennan expanded."

"She's the best we have and you know it. I got Eliza Rose on board."

"Of course you did." I sighed and mumbled that my brother was an asshole. "Look I get it, you're the edgy one and I'm the boring one, but this is reckless, even for you. Something happens to us, I'll make your afterlife a living hell no matter where we end up. Got it?"

Sage hummed. "Us, huh? See you in two hours, Oh Boring One."

"Fuck a drink, you owe me a bottle, Knullare. See you in two." I hung up and threw on some jeans, then tried my very last attempt to stop the madness. I called Brennan. "Bror, have you heard from our lovely, bearded brother today?"

My tone was filled with sarcasm and Brenn absolutely picked up on it. "I already tried to talk him out of it, but he makes some good points."

"Did he?" I froze. "What were those, exactly? I must have missed them when I was calmly yelling at him."

"Like the fact that this place wouldn't be shit without him, and the fact that letting him do things his own way keeps our overhead low enough that we can afford models like Eliza Rose and still have more money than God," Brenn reminded me. "Whether either of us want to admit it, Sage is bar-none the best in the business. Also, he threw the whole 'consenting adults' thing in my face."

"Consent is overrated." I frowned at myself and shook my head. "That came out wrong. You didn't hear me say that, ja? Fuck, alright. Sage is the best in the biz and I'm going too, so … yeah. Tell Mor I love her. After, though. She'll freak out if she knows beforehand."

"It's better for everyone if she never knows anything at all," he muttered. "Out of curiosity though, why are you going, exactly? I've never known you to care about Sage's ridiculousness."

It's not about him. "I always care, I'm just never privy to what's happening until after it's happened and the only reason I know now is because Nila is going with them."

"Oh, right. Nila. That makes sense. Just be careful, okay?"

"Always am … or I normally am. Guess I kinda lose my head where Nila's concerned. That uh, normal?" I scratched my head, only feeling slightly awkward at the admission.

"Do you understand how many children I have?" he deadpanned. "Yes, it's normal to completely lose your fucking head when you're in love. And don't give me that 'just friends' shit, either. You look at her the way Sage looks at spaghetti sandwiches."

I snorted. "Hel, it's that bad? Guess I'm not as slick as I thought I was. Speaking of kids, are you guys done, or are three boys not enough?"

"She wants a girl. So, we'll be done when she says we're done." He sighed quietly as his chair groaned loudly enough to be audible. "It's not like I'm capable of saying no to her."

I couldn't help but grin and make an ill-timed joke I knew would piss him off. "Love how she put you in your place."

"Laugh all you want. Nila's already got you in yours," he countered. "Let me guess … you tried to say no, she batted her eyelashes and now all of a sudden you're heading out in a storm tonight?"

I deserved that. "For the record, it was over the phone, so I don't have a clue what her eyelashes were doing, but oh, look, I'm going through a tunnel … I … you … fuck off." I hung up with an eye-roll and started searching for a shirt. That wasn't one of my finest moments, but sometimes it was hard to be mature when you had five brothers.

Within twenty minutes I was getting in the car and heading over to Eldan International, but I made sure to grab lunch from Nila's favorite fast food joint to ensure she got food in her belly. I handed it over the second she climbed in the car. "Eat."

"Yes, Sir." She winked at me as she popped a fry into her mouth, like she hadn't just fucking slayed me with two little words, and I had a serious 'am I into this' argument in my head.

What was going on in my upstairs head didn't truly matter anyway, because my downstairs head was absolutely fucking into it and I had to remember what the hell we were doing there to get him to shut up. The entire internal crisis lasted about five whole minutes and I didn't miss the way she was staring at me while she ate. *Fuck, say something not weird. Uhh…* "Duktig flicka." *Good girl?! Really!*

"Did you just call me an asshole again?" she asked, pinching her brows together as she chewed. "Rude."

"No." My grip tightened on the steering wheel. "I said 'good girl.'"

Her lips parted as she squirmed, and I could see it in every line of her body, in the look in her eyes … she needed that. "Oh. I take back what I said, then. It's not rude at all."

I slid my hand over to grip her thigh, then leaned in to bite the fry out of her fingers as I smiled. "Good."

"So … so you're a fan of that, huh?" she asked, pupils wide and voice strained. "Being obeyed? I had my suspicions, but …"

"I mean yeah, I just haven't gone into all that too much. Have you?"

She shook her head. "You mean besides Clay's basement? No. Most guys don't earn it. They like to boss me around but I've never met anyone I'd listen to … other than you."

I smiled, leaning over to kiss her cheek. "I listen to you too, sweetheart. I think it should always go both ways." I contemplated that and wiggled my hand in an unsure manner. "Sometimes. Maybe not always in bed."

"Think you're gonna keep bossing me around in bed, huh?" she asked, eyes dancing. "I'm gonna need more fries for that."

"You got it. All the fries you need and more." I started toward Sage's house with a soft smile, my hand still firmly on her thigh. "You know I'm fucking you tonight, right, Nila?"

"Promise?" She spread her legs for me and bit her lip, slowly dragging my hand a little higher. "I'm on birth control and I got tested two weeks ago. Just throwing that out there."

"Are you saying …" My vision blurred as I connected the puzzle pieces, and she absolutely just gave me permission to come inside her. "I've been tested since my last too. Fuck this shoot, I want you now."

"Patience, T. We've waited this long." She closed her legs and moved my hand, lacing our fingers and gently reminding me that we were in a moving car going eighty miles an hour, which meant I needed to pay attention to where we were going.

The skies were already dark and threatening rain, making me nervous all over again as we got to Sage's and jumped in his Rover for a short drive to the trees behind his house.

If we die today and I never get to fuck my best friend, I really will kick Sage's ass in the afterlife.

FOURTEEN

Earth, Wind, and a Fucking Tornado

It started pouring before we reached the trees, making me curse in annoyance at my brother. "Great. How are you supposed to get any photos in pouring rain?"

He ignored me completely as he glanced at his phone, so I took a moment to look around. Sage had lived in the same house since he'd been old enough to move out — off the beaten path, much smaller than the rest of ours, with a detached garage and enough land to build a farm. I couldn't see much through the rain coating the Range Rover's windows, but I knew enough to know he'd never brought me out this far back. We'd gone through a field easily a half-mile long and stopped at a line of trees for Sage to get his shit together and Nila to do Eliza's makeup, and I was a little apprehensive about what we'd find on the other side.

"Okay, just hang tight," Sage said as he started digging through his bag. "You guys ready?"

"Just about. Isn't she gorgeous?" Nila shifted a little so we could see her better as Eliza laughed.

Sage eyed her like he thought 'gorgeous' was an understatement. "Absolutely. Now, some ground rules. Don't go running off unless you have to. I'm gonna leave the keys in here just in case, but we should stick together. We get in, get set up, I'll take around two dozen shots … and then we hightail it back to my house. Everybody got that?"

"Yep." Nila leaned forward and pushed the back of my head. "Got it."

I faked a scoff and tried to keep my mind from picturing what I was going to do to her later for that little show. "Apparently my little brother is the boss here."

Eliza chimed in, "I don't think I met a Novak that wasn't bossy, honestly. Sage is probably the least bos— never mind, Archie is."

Sage and I exchanged glances. She didn't know how right she was. "Okay. Time to go," he said suddenly.

All at once, the rain stopped, and Nila swore under her breath. "How'd you do that?"

"Viking secret," Sage teased, sounding like he was damn proud of himself. "Come on, we don't have much time."

I got out of the car against every instinct I had, then helped Nila out of the backseat and grabbed an umbrella. Once Sage had everything he needed, we made our way through the line of trees and came out the other side to a second large field — and this one was home to the most dilapidated, rotting barn I'd ever seen.

Sage yelled orders to the three of us like he honestly believed he *was* in charge. "Let's get a couple without rain and then just see what happens."

"Definitely not scared of a little rain," Eliza said, but Nila was glaring at the clouds in a way that made me shudder. I knew that look, and it was one that I never wanted to be on the other side of.

We only got through a handful of shots before it started raining again and it got so fucking windy that the umbrella flew right out of my hands. Within seconds after that, the first true clap of thunder shook the trees. It came on so suddenly that it felt like the storm had formed right on top of our heads, and still, none of us moved. My idiot brother stayed to take shots of the background, so I turned to Nila and pulled her in closer. "Fuck this, we need to get to Sage's basement as soon as possible."

She hesitated for a moment, until thunder crashed again and she nearly lost her balance from the wind, then nodded quickly. "You don't need to tell me twice," she rushed out.

Sage came sprinting over with his camera shoved under his shirt to protect it from the sideways rain and yelled, "Toby! Tobias! Take Nila back to the car and go to the house!"

"I was just telling her that. You're coming too. Don't be insane, Bror," I begged, getting even more desperate when lightning struck a little too close.

"You're right. Go, I'll get Eliza!" He turned and tried to get Eliza's attention, and I knew that would have to be good enough.

I grabbed Nila's hand and started running back through the trees. The wind was so fast I could feel a resistance with every step, and seeing even a foot in front of us was difficult. We didn't say much as we dodged bushes and branches at every turn, but when we saw Sage's car it felt like a light at the end of a tunnel — only that light was promptly put out when a tree came crashing down on top of it.

Nila's scream had me feeling like a caged animal, and I glanced back to see where Sage was and saw nothing but the storm. *He's okay. It's fucking Sage, just get Nila to safety.* I tugged her hand and started running again, my eyes searching for any sort of shelter as we ran the half a mile back toward Sage's house. "Come on!" I yelled when I spotted it, hope flourishing in my chest as the faint sound of barking reached my ears.

We were drenched and exhausted when we entered the house. Sage's dog Heimdall was jumping on us and whimpering as I slammed the door and prayed to every God I could think of that Sage was behind us. "It's right here, we have to get downstairs. Come on, Heimdall! We made it, Niles. Now we just have to wait for Sage. Did you see him behind us at all?"

I yanked open his heavy storm door and led them down as she shook her head and tried to wring the water out of her hair. "No, I couldn't see shit out there."

"Me either." I knew my prepared brother would have some rations down there and was pleased to find some towels. It was much quieter as I draped one of them over her shoulders and pulled her in for a hug. "This shit is crazy."

"You think?" She held me tightly and buried her face in my neck. "I'm sorry, T. I should've listened."

"It's not your fault, you have to know that." I kissed her forehead and took a breath, then glanced at the stairs. "Where the fuck is he?"

"Knowing Sage, he's probably trying to saddle the damn storm so he can ride it," she mumbled. "I'm sure he'll be here any second."

I huffed, closing my eyes for one last prayer. "You're not wrong. Fuck, I'm sorry this happened. But we're alive, and we'll be home in a few hours and have a sleepover in the living room. How's that sound?"

"Sounds perfect." She kissed my chin and then my neck, just once, and then I heard the sirens.

It felt like a horror movie being played in slow motion as my brain processed what that noise was, and then I couldn't fucking breathe. "A fucking tornado! Fuck, fuck, fuck!" I started to pace, glaring at the door like I'd kill it if it didn't open and reveal my brother safe, and Nila's hands tightened in my soaked shirt.

"Toby, no. It's Sage, wherever he is, he's fine!" she said quickly, trying to pull my attention back to her. "We do as he said and stay here."

"And if he's not fine?" I asked, desperate to hear her tell me he'd be okay, like she could see the future. "He was supposed to be right behind us." *What if he's not okay and I left him out there?* The guilt would eat me alive.

"He's … he's Sage. He knows this land better than anyone, and he's not alone. It's all gonna be okay, T." Nila hugged me tighter, but as we heard the sound of breaking glass and another tree falling, I knew what I had to do.

"I have to go look, sweetheart. I have to see how bad it is out there. Just stay with Heimdall, if the tornado is still touching land I won't leave the house."

She looked at me like I was insane — certifiably, completely insane — but I could see the moment when she realized I wasn't going to budge on this. "What if something happens to you?" she whispered.

I didn't know how to answer that for a moment. "Sage has a landline. As soon as the sirens stop, call for help. I won't run into a tornado, okay? I know there's nothing I can do there. I just — fuck, I have to know. I know Sage is resilient, but he's still my little brother."

"I know. Please don't die." She grabbed my face and kissed me fully, deeply, then shoved me toward the stairs. "Bring them back."

"I will." I stared into her gorgeous blue eyes as I backpedaled away. She was so fucking strong, and although I knew I could be making a huge mistake, she gave me the push I needed. "Sleepover tonight, I promise."

I forced myself to turn away and dart up the stairs. Nila was safe with Heimdall and my little brother needed me. It didn't matter how big and outdoorsy he was, he would always be my little brother, and if something happened to him while I was a half a mile away, I just didn't think I'd be able to live with myself after that.

The metal door was a bitch to shove open with the wind pushing through a broken window, but nothing could have prepared me for the noise once I was firmly on the other side of it. Sage's belongings were blown all around the house: there were shards of glass on the floor, books tossed feet away from the bookshelf, and a terrifying whistling that I feared would live in my brain forever. There was absolutely a tornado happening outside. I hoped it wasn't as close as I feared, but when I opened the front door and a gust of wind slapped the air from my lungs, I knew I was fucked.

My brother was fucked.

It spun around in that field like I was in the middle of a *Storm Chasers* episode, ripping trees from the ground and blocking me from getting anywhere near the barn — if the barn even still stood. I fell to my knees and tried to breathe. Ice-cold fear spread through my veins like I had shot myself up with it as I imagined my brother out there, being tossed around like a rag doll, but the screams I released might as well have been silent compared to that godforsaken whistling. I screamed his name, eyes scanning anywhere and everywhere in hopes of seeing him, but with the rain and wind it was impossible. It was so dark outside, it was like the sun had abandoned us … and for a few moments I believed it had.

As the last of my hope drained from me, I found my footing and slammed the door, making my way back to Nila in a daze as a deep sense of failure settled in my stomach. I'd come to this shoot to protect her, but a big part of me had known I'd be protecting my brother too if it came down to it. Instead, I'd only managed to do half my job, and the half I'd failed could destroy the last bit of strength my mother had.

Nila's face was pale as I made my way downstairs, and to my surprise, she didn't ask me anything. She just pulled me in and held me, letting me feel whatever it was I needed to feel, and I could never express what that did for me. She was everything I needed and more.

Minutes felt like hours as I stayed curled up in her arms, and when the wind finally slowed and an odd sense of calm spread around us, I couldn't find it in me to move. Down there, I could pretend Sage was fine and convince myself that he'd found a way to bunker down, but if I went up top and that wasn't the case, I'd have to accept the fact that my little brother was gone. I just couldn't do that.

Her voice was small as it comforted me, assured me that my brother was okay and reminded me that we were alive, but nothing snapped me out of it until I heard the loud bang of a door and the stomping of boots on Sage's hardwood floor. "Sage?" I whispered, meeting Nila's eyes to make sure she heard it too. More stomping confirmed it. "Sage!"

"I'm here! Toby!"

Heimdall started barking like crazy as I took the steps two at a time, and when I finally saw Sage for myself, I launched myself at him and nearly tackled him in a bear hug.

"Fucking Hel, I thought I lost you! Godsdamnit, Bror." For a moment I didn't think I'd ever let him go, but then I remembered he wasn't alone. "Eliza?"

"She hurt her ankle badly enough that she couldn't walk, so I took her to the barn. Fucking roof is gone, and the door too … but I wanna find the guy that constructed those walls and kiss him right on the mouth," Sage muttered. "They fucking held."

Nila moved past us both to check on Eliza. "I need hazard pay if I'm going to keep working for you Novaks," she said. "I nearly lost an eye trying to stop him from running out into a tornado after you."

She wasn't wrong, but my dumb ass still tried to do it. "She's exaggerating. Her eyes were completely safe."

"I'm sure they were," Sage said sarcastically. "I'm gonna call an ambulance to get her checked out. Is your car okay? I didn't even notice."

"I don't know. Yours was fucked. We had to run the whole way here and Heimdall was going crazy so I just grabbed him and brought him down to wait on you. I'll go check the cars, cell service is probably fucked too."

I relaxed and watched him a second longer before I went to actually check outside. It really didn't matter what hell was waiting for us out there — cars or no cars, we'd survived.

That was truly all that mattered.

FIFTEEN

Say It Again

I did my best not to think of that tornado once we were safe at home, but I couldn't help it. Any loud bang had me looking for Nila to ensure she was okay, and those helpless feelings in the basement would come rushing back. But for the most part, I just didn't think about it. I didn't talk about it, and I damn sure didn't want to dream about it.

Not that my subconscious gave a shit.

I knew it would happen, I'd just hoped I'd have a little time before I was traumatized all over again, not a measly couple of days.

"Niles, I have to go out there. Just stay here with Heimdall and don't open that door."

She moved between me and the door, shaking her head with tears in her eyes. "No! Toby, you can't! They're too far, you have to trust him!"

"Trust him? It doesn't matter if I trust him, he's my little brother. I have to protect him," I pleaded, not wanting to move her out of the way.

"By dying?" she yelled. "Toby, please! There's nothing you can do, they'll be okay. They'll be here any minute, I'm sure of it."

"He's got three minutes to open that door, or I'm going after him." I paced, wringing out my hands like I did as a child when I was nervous, but this time it did nothing to calm me. Three minutes came and went, and I could see how on edge I was making Nila. Just as I began to feel bad about it, I heard a loud crash inside the house making me dart up those stairs and slam into the door … only it didn't budge. "Fucking Hel, it won't open! Sage!!"

"Toby!" She ran up behind me, tugging me back by my shirt. I nearly elbowed her in the face

as I stumbled back down a step, but she dodged and somehow ended up in front of me. "You can't do this. Please don't leave me."

It was probably the only thing that could have snapped me out of it. I pulled her in and held her, telling her I wouldn't leave her and that I was right there. "I just don't want that door jammed. The storm will clear, and we still have to get out, Niles. I won't leave you, okay?"

She clung to me as the sound of shattering glass filled the house, and I moved around her to look around for something we could use to bust it down — anything at all — but found nothing. There was nothing to help me, nothing to help her, so I threw all my body weight at that door and screamed my brother's name. "Sage! Sage! Sa—"

That screaming is ultimately what woke me, and I sat up in my bed and yelled for my best friend without realizing.

"Nila!"

Twenty seconds later, she was opening my door and closing her open robe. "Toby? What's wrong? What happened?"

"Fuck." I ran a hand through my hair and sighed. "Bad dream. Are you okay?" I got up to check on her anyway, my brain still groggy and trying to cling to anything solid.

She stepped easily into my arms, letting me touch her familiar curves. "I'm fine. I'm okay, I'm right here."

For a few moments, all I did was hold her. I didn't fully trust my mouth yet, but when I did, I decided to talk about it for the first time. "Have you dreamt about it?"

"Oh," she said softly. "Yeah, I have. Couple of times. Did you?"

I nodded, squeezing a little tighter. "That was my first one. How accurate are yours?"

"Not accurate, usually. Just the same feelings and setting." She kissed the corner of my mouth and nuzzled into my neck. "Do you want to tell me about it?"

I shook my head but spoke anyway. "I couldn't get out of the room. We were trapped in there and it sounded like the whole house was being destroyed."

"We're safe, T. You kept me safe and Sage did the smart thing. Our house is fine." Her lips pressed against my neck and I slowly started backing toward my bed without loosening my grip.

I needed her.

"Stay. Please."

"Not going anywhere." We tumbled onto the bed with her laying half on top of me and me just letting the smell of her calm me down. She was here, she was real, and she was mine … almost.

"Thank you," I murmured, then admitted out loud what I'd been telling myself over and over. "I need you."

I let her decide what it meant, because I needed her in so many ways I couldn't pick which one. She responded by slowly, carefully, raising her face to meet my eyes, then kissing me gently. "Take me, T. I'm yours. I'm right here, and I'm yours."

In one movement I had our positions switched and I was staring down at her in the moonlight shining through the window, my cock waking instantly as I slotted between her legs. "You're so beautiful, Nila."

She gasped as I hooked one finger in the tie of her robe and undid it, and as it fell open, I got my first true look at her. "Still think so?" she whispered, bending her legs and caging me between them.

I stared in awe, my hand sliding along her skin as the need to touch all of her took hold, and I nodded without any trace of doubt. "Every inch of you." I kissed my way down her neck to her breasts, flicking a nipple with my tongue to make her arch her back.

"I've wanted you since the day I first laid eyes on you, T. Please don't make me wait anymore."

Her hands snaked down to push my boxers off and I nearly ripped them as I tried to assist her. I rubbed the head of my cock along her pelvis and thighs, breathing heavily when my brain processed what we were about to do. I was finally going to fuck my best friend, a woman I'd craved for years … a woman I was in love with.

When I circled my cock on her clit we moaned together, both desperate for me to go just a little further down, and as torturous as it was, I stayed there a few seconds more. I didn't want to rush it, I wanted to take my time with her, but when I slid between her lips and felt how wet she was, I lost all my resolve and shoved the tip inside. "Oh fuck, Niles. So fucking hot."

"Tobias, please!" she begged, rocking her hips and digging her nails into my skin. "I can't — I can't wait another fucking second."

Her lips crashed against mine as her tongue slid into my mouth and I bottomed out completely. We laid there just like that for a while, me deep inside her with our mouths locked together in a heated kiss, and then I started to move. Nila was by far the best thing I'd ever felt in my life and I knew exactly why. "I got you, sweetheart. I'm here, fuck, I — I love you."

"Toby." She melted into my mattress as she slung her arms around my neck to pin me to her, and her ankles hooked behind my ass as she started riding me from below. "Say it again," she moaned. "Please."

"I love you." I said it with no doubt and a small smile. "Love you so fucking much, you're mine. Only mine now."

The reminder that I didn't have to share her anymore had my hips snapping a little faster, making her lips part beautifully and her cheeks blush in pleasure. "I love you too."

Those words had me kissing her again, but not just her mouth. I kissed all over her face and neck until I was sucking a small, territorial mark at the base and drilling myself into her. "Duktig flicka. Now come for me. Come on your man's cock like you've been dying for him."

"Oh god," she rushed out, "I'm your good girl!" Her body bowed as her head tipped back and her eyes rolled, and she didn't just come on my cock, she soaked it. Her pussy clenched tight and hot and wouldn't let me go even as I started to slip out. I made sure to shove back inside and grind against her, reaching up to grip her chin as I watched her vision return.

"You are my good girl. You got one more in there for me?"

She nodded quickly and whimpered a yes, staring at me with those beautifully ice-blue eyes all wide under pinched brows. "Always, Sir. Are you gonna come inside me?"

I twitched right alongside my cock and nearly stopped moving all together. "Hell yeah I am, sweetheart. Gonna fill you up and mark you mine, but first you're going to give me one more. Rub your clit for me, let me watch how you like to touch yourself."

"God, I love when you talk like that!" She shifted and spread herself open, rubbing with three fingers as she rocked her thick hips, and I held myself there so she could fuck herself on my cock.

I'd seen the northern lights in Sweden, sunsets from Hawaii to Dublin; I'd seen the Great Ocean Road in Australia and gorgeous models in every shape, size and ethnicity. None of it could compare to her. "Give it to me, Nila. Your orgasm is mine."

"Toby …"

She bucked her hips, losing all rhythm as she took what she needed from me and free-fell over that ledge. She was so wet, so tight and hot and welcome and *mine* that I couldn't fight it anymore.

I dropped down to take what *I* needed and groaned in her ear how good she felt. "I love you, fuck I'm gonna come. Gonna fill up your pussy —" I slammed deep inside and let go, body trembling with a release that changed my entire outlook on life. This was how it should have always felt.

"God, I feel it," she whispered, letting out a tiny, perfect growl. "I've — I've never been able to feel it before."

I smiled, unable to help myself. "The Novak seed is strong."

"What the fuck," she laughed, shoving me back just a little. "Way to ruin a perfectly good moment, Tobias."

Despite the words, her grin hadn't ever been that bright, and I was sure mine hadn't either. I stayed inside her and melted into her neck, making a home there with a sleepy hum. "Moment's still perfect for me. I got you."

"It's about time." She squeezed me, letting her legs relax. "I was starting to fear we'd never get here, T. Thought we'd slipped a little too far into the friendzone … but I don't ever wanna go back. You're it for me."

Knowing she felt exactly how I did helped ease any fears I had. "You're it for me too, you've *been* it for me. I haven't been with anyone else in a long time. I've only wanted you. We can't go back, you're my best friend and you're my woman."

"Good. Then kiss me and let me up so I can pee, then I'll come back here and sleep with you tonight. No more nightmares, okay?"

"No more nightmares, sweetheart. Hurry back." I watched her go, feeling on top of the world. I knew there was no world where I didn't pine for her, but at least in this one I got to have her as my own. She would always be my number one girl.

SIXTEEN

Never Too Late for a Second Date

"Earth to Tobes," Sage called seconds before throwing the basketball at my head. Luckily for me, I caught it, because as always when we played basketball at the park, we had a small crowd. They weren't there for me, I knew they were there for the twins, but that didn't change the fact that they *were* there and I didn't want a crowd seeing me get blitzed in the face.

It was me and Sage against Kale and Kai, and just seeing them on a team and working together settled something in my chest. They really were getting better, even if they bickered every time Sage or I scored a basket. One cool thing about having so many brothers was things like this — we had friends for life, close ones, and because of that we didn't need many friends outside of each other. Partners were a different story obviously, but besides a very few friends who we all held close, we were normally good just hanging with each other. I fucking hated heights, so basketball was one of the safer choices, even if I occasionally had to go hiking with Sage to get him off my back. We hadn't done anything since the tornado though, and I had to admit … I missed him.

When we took a quick water break, I finally had an opportunity to ask him how he'd been, and when he glanced around us, I could tell he was glad the twins were off talking shit about Kai's neighbor.

"I'm alive. Still feel like shit about Eliza's ankle, but she's slowly getting better. What about you and Nila? You guys okay?"

I told him we were fine and nearly spilled all the beans, but I decided I wanted to do that with Nila by my side. At least with everyone but Kale, and that was only because I'd already slipped that we'd kissed to him.

He waited until we were done playing basketball to ask, and when he followed me to my car I already knew it was coming, so I rushed it out before he could. "Things are great, yes we've kissed more, yes we've gone further than that, and no you don't get details like you freely give."

Kale laughed annoyingly. "I was going to ask if you were coming to dinner at Mor's this weekend, but thanks for the update. Who are you talking about again?" I knew he was joking, but it didn't stop me from slapping him upside the head, only making him laugh harder. "Right, the only one that gets you all … Brennan-like. Good, I'm happy for you. Maybe you'll come together?"

He looked so hopeful, I forgot he was a married adult for a second and saw nothing but my baby brother. "Maybe. Stop looking at me like that. Why do you care about my love life anyway?"

"I don't care about your love life, I'm not Archie. I care about your happiness, and if you'd rather fuck a doll or never fuck again, I'd just want you to be happy."

I almost interrupted him and brought up something he was embarrassed about, but I decided to leave cantaloupes out of the conversation and thank him instead. "Thanks. I'm happy. Now at least … she's mine."

Kale's smile made me think he had more Archie in him than he'd ever admit, but I could tell he really was happy for me. Of course, I also saw the moment he was going to ruin it. "What was the sex like the first time? You last longer than a minute?"

"And Kale's back. Fuck off, Bror. I'll see you this weekend." I shoved his face away, jumped in my car before he could respond and rushed home to shower.

JENSEN

~

Nila and I had been on plenty of dates before, but none of them were like this. She was my girl, and I was now able to hold her hand and kiss her whenever I wanted to. This was our first real date, and I had to make it a good one. I had an idea that I knew she'd love, but that one was going to take more time and planning on my part to get it set up, so for now I was settling on a complete redo of when we should have begun.

Unfortunately going to a beach couldn't be a surprise since she needed to dress accordingly, so I gave her that much before we dressed and left out the fact that we'd be having dinner on the balcony during the sunset. Maybe that was cheesy, but I was determined to make her forget all those losers before me, and I knew how much my girl loved the sunset over the water.

"Ready?" I called, packing up some waters and towels for us.

"Is anyone ever ready for a date with a Novak?" she quipped, coming around the corner in a white bikini that slayed me. "Can you tie this for me? I can't ever seem to get it tight enough to hold my boobs up by myself."

"These shorts do nothing to hide a boner, baby. But here …" I moved behind her and tied it tight for her, then kissed the back of her neck. "Just you and me, okay? We're still us. I just get to do this now." I placed a soft but firm slap to her ass, then swallowed my damn heart as she glanced back over her shoulder at me with a look that said she was ready to test me.

"Oh? You wanna spank me, baby? Maybe we should play a little today, then."

"I like games. I always win." I pulled her in by her chin but stopped short of kissing her. "What kind of game?"

She hummed, poking her tongue out between her teeth. "You get to spank me once for every person who checks me out today. And I get five seconds of your mouth for everyone who checks you out."

"Fuck," I whispered, my cock throbbing so hard I knew she felt it. "Absolutely. But you're going to get a lot of spankings in this outfit, Niles."

"Maybe I chose it for a reason. We have a lot of time to make up for, T. And I'm banking you'll be eating me out for at least an hour, so … I win both ways." She winked, rocking up to kiss me before dropping back down and grabbing her sarong from the back of the couch. "Load up, big guy. Our second date awaits."

"Second, huh?" I slapped her ass again and followed, nearly forgetting the bag I'd packed as I watched her hips sway, but I darted back before we reached the door.

"Yeah. The one you forgot to invite me to, remember?" She hopped in my car and stretched her giant, ridiculous straw hat over her lap. "Better late than never, I guess."

"I don't know why, but I love when you lay out in the sun with that stupid hat.

More beautiful than any model in the world. I'll stand by that statement until I die." I turned on my gorgeous classic car and put it in reverse, the noise lulling us into a comfortable silence, and once we were firmly on the road I reached over and placed a hand on her thigh.

She hummed along to the radio as she pulled my hand up a little higher, and I found myself wondering how long she'd really wanted this … how many times we'd touched and it did more for her than I knew.

When we got to the beach, I knew we both would have happily fucked right there in my car, but this date was important for us. I leaned over for a quick kiss and got out, walking around to open her door and help her straighten her hat. "Ready to earn some spankings?"

"I never thought I'd say this, but yes." She swung those intoxicating hips as she tugged me along, and I was pretty sure she'd already earned three by the time we found a spot to set up our towels. "You going in the water with me?"

"Yeah, first I'm going to put sunblock on your gorgeous skin. Then yes, I will." I sat behind her and grabbed the bottle from the bag, chuckling as she cursed me under her breath. As long as I'd known her, she'd hated the way sunblock felt on her skin — but I had a feeling she'd change her mind now.

Sure enough, I barely had her shoulders covered before she was groaning quietly. "Fuck. I've craved your hands for so long, I don't know if I can do this. Be careful where you touch me."

"Is that a challenge?" I whispered into her ear, leaning in to kiss her neck and start on her lower back.

"It wasn't, but … fuck. Don't stop," she breathed. "I don't know how I ever survived you."

I knew she meant our friendship, the lines we'd drawn, the times we'd held back, and I honestly didn't know how we'd done it either. I finished putting the cream everywhere the sun touched, including her adorable little nose, and then I hastily rubbed some on my arms as a last-minute thought. "Race you to the water."

"Aww, hell." She pushed herself up and tossed her sarong on the towel, then darted toward the water — but I was faster.

I made it there and spun around just in time to splash her, then pulled her in for a quick apology kiss. "Want to get on my back?"

"Not quite." She pushed me into the water, then wrapped her arms and legs around me, kissing me again and again as her hat shielded us both from the world. "Love you, T. This isn't bad for a date I had to wait like a decade for."

I chuckled, holding her there and trying and failing to hold her ass cheeks with each palm. I noticed three people looking in a matter of seconds and decided to give her an update. "I love you too, sweetheart. But guess your number so far."

"Mmm… do you count? If so, then one," she said, biting her lower lip. "This beach is empty, I don't see anyone else."

"Nice answer." I leaned in to nibble her chin and neck, then spit out the taste of sunblock with a grin. "Yep, I put too much."

She brushed her thumb over my lips and smiled softly. "How many?"

"Eight so far, one had to get the look before he stopped staring. Might have to kick someone's ass, Nila."

"Nah. Just spank mine." She put her hat on my head then swam backward, letting the water rush over her body until she was flipping over and diving under. I watched her long hair trail behind her and had a moment of disbelief, where I couldn't understand how I got her. Still, I wasn't going to torture myself with whether I deserved her or not; I was just going to do everything in my power to keep her.

I wore her hat proudly until she was done swimming, then helped her wring out her hair and tie it behind her once again. Finally, I pulled her in so she was facing the water while I held her. "Dinner is soon, the sky is already changing."

"A sunset dinner? Tobias Novak, who knew you were romantic?" She turned to kiss me, and I shook my head before giving her what she craved.

"You knew. I'm only this way with you, and I'll always be this for you. I'm just going to also fart in your blankets and wrestle you after you beat me in Call of Duty."

"Yeah? How would that go? You pin me down and … what, exactly?" she asked. "Tell me, T."

I knew what she was doing, and I was one hundred percent here for it. "First I'd grab your legs and tug so you'd go flat on your back, then I'd climb on top of you and pin you there until you said you were sorry, all while grinding my cock against your clothed pussy."

She clenched, sucking in a quiet breath. "And if I didn't say I was sorry?"

"Then I wouldn't stop until I was coming all over your pajamas and pulsing with my head pressed against your clit, and you wouldn't come until you said it." With the water blocking most of us I reached around and pressed her magic button. "Right here."

"Fuck me sideways, that's hot." She laughed a little breathlessly, then kissed me deeply. "Let's go eat. Sex in the ocean is a terrible idea."

"You got it sweetheart. Let me show you how this should have gone years ago."

I helped her out of the water, and once we were dry and reasonably clothed again, we had that dinner overlooking the sunset. Or at least, I was pretty sure we did — I couldn't see anything but her. I lost count of how many people glanced her way, of how long we sat there laughing and feeding each other even after darkness set, and suddenly, I was glad it had taken me so long to get there.

I hadn't been ready for her, for this, back in high school or the years immediately after, but I was ready for her now … and she was worth the wait.

SEVENTEEN

Death By Parties

Work without Nila there was boring. I never saw her while we were there anyway, but still, just knowing she was close helped the day go faster.

Knowing she was at home was a million times worse. It was impossible to have her here in three minutes so I could taste her, and impossible to sink inside her with my hand over her mouth before my meeting with Brennan. *Great, now I'm hard and I want to watch her touch herself.* But I grinned as something very possible came to mind; I just needed to be patient.

Me: *What you doing, beautiful?*

The dots appeared immediately.

Niles: *Just cleaning and making more messes. How's work?*

Me: *Shitty without you. Plus …*

I sent a picture of my tented slacks and then another message before she could respond.

Me: *Put your vibrator in for me, sweetheart.*

Niles: *Yes, Tobias. Give me five.*

She followed up three minutes later with a picture of it disappearing inside of her, and my cock jumped so hard I grunted. "Fucking Hel, I'm going to kill myself with this."

Me: *Duktig flicka. Put your panties back on and go back to what you were doing.*

The "Yes, Tobias" she sent back went directly south, and I was impatient enough for the first half of my plan that I instantly went into the app and pressed the button. I closed my eyes and imagined her face when she felt it. I messed with the speed for a moment and then turned it off, my fingers slamming down on the keyboard as I sent off an email.

I was dying by the time I sat down in the meeting room, my attention so far away that Brennan had to call my name multiple times whenever someone asked me a question. This was exactly why I'd worked the night shift for so many years. I hated meetings with a burning passion — my mind always wandered too much. I made it through the conference only to be asked to stay back by Brenn, but he let me go when I told him I was horny.

He didn't want those details.

The only good thing about any of it was having that app in my hand, and the amount of times I had pressed it surely had her dying at home. I was excited to call her when I was finally back in my office and alone.

"Hey, baby. How you doing?"

She sounded out of breath as she whispered, "You're murdering me, T. You know that, right? When the cops come find my body, you're going to get arrested."

"You're strong, baby. I know you got this, just breathe. How wet are you right now?"

"Panties are soaked … can't walk without feeling it over my thighs," she mumbled. "Don't think I can get wetter without actually coming."

My hands clenched at the visual, imagining how it would be to reach in there and feel it for myself. I needed it. "Bring me your panties, Nila. Don't take them off until you get here."

She swore under her breath and then moaned, but told me she'd be there soon — and I couldn't do anything but pace my office and remind myself I was playing a long game today until she arrived.

The flowy, dark green dress she was wearing when she walked in had me stopping dead in my tracks, and my heart nearly stopped too when she slid out of her panties and handed them over to me.

"I have a clean pair in my purse. Do you want me to put them on, or leave them off?" she asked, trembling slightly.

"Put them on so I have more later." I kissed her before she could let go of the panties and then immediately brought them to my nose. She could see how hard it made me, and I let her watch my pupils blow at her scent. "Smell so fucking good, sweetheart."

Nila's breathing picked up as she stepped in a little closer. "Never thought that would be so hot, but fuck, T. You really like it that much?"

I nodded without an ounce of doubt. "I love it. Makes me so hard I can hardly think about anything but bending you over my desk and fucking you."

"So why don't you?" She closed the distance and pulled her bottom lip between her teeth, then nodded to my desk. "It's right there, I'm right here … I'm desperate for you, baby."

My breath hitched in my throat as I reached out to grab her and bend her over it. "Desperate for me?" I rubbed my erection against her ass. "Do you feel what you do to me?"

"Toby, please!" she moaned, rocking back and grinding against me. "Just pull my dress up and take me."

I kept her dress where it was and continued to rub myself against her while I sniffed her delicious panties. "I could come just like this."

"Fuck. Fucking hell, T. That's hot as hell but there's … there's no way," she challenged.

I sneered and kept grinding against her, my plan to edge with her panties going straight out the window. "No? You don't think I'll come all over your dress and just go right back to work?"

She jerked, squirming until I pinned her to my desk, then let out a huff. "Do it, baby. Use me. Please."

I knew she needed this as badly as I did — my Nila could handle being edged all day, but only if she knew she was bringing me pleasure. I inhaled her panties again and started grinding harder, groaning and sliding my hands along her ass and hips. I knew I couldn't get come on my slacks, so I moved back just enough to shove them down, then slotted myself between her cheeks. "Dress is soft, baby. You know I'll take good care of you tonight, you're so good for me."

"I know," she rushed out, dropping her forehead to her arm. "You have to turn it off. The vibe, I … Toby, I'll come if you don't."

The quiet, intermittent buzz reminded me that I had, in fact, forgotten all about the vibe, so I stilled to reach over for my phone and turned it off. "We're not done there yet, but for now, this is about what I need, huh, sweetheart?"

"Yes, Sir." Her voice was stronger now as she adjusted herself and lifted her ass just a little higher for me. "Use me."

Those words *"use me"* echoed in my brain as I did exactly that, her panties pressed to my nose and my body pressed to hers. It was glorious. "Fuck, I love you. You're so perfect. This ass is so perfect."

She grunted and moved with me, rocking so my cock slid between her cheeks and nudged the soft fabric of her dress, over and over again until I was pulling her head back by her hair and growling in her ear. "Gonna fucking come, Niles. Gonna ruin this beautiful fucking dre—" I couldn't even finish the word before my cock was jumping and painting the green on her ass white.

"How the hell was that so hot?" she whispered, rolling her hips again to make me twitch. "I want it inside me later, though. Promise me, T. And promise you won't be gentle."

I huffed a laugh, placing one firm slap on her ass before I backed away. "Not a chance. Need a picture of you like this, okay?"

She agreed quickly, so I snapped one from my eye level then dropped to my knees, lifting her ruined dress enough to see her dripping pussy squeezing that vibe. Her skin was shiny with how wet she was, her thighs shaking, and I knew I'd never seen anything better.

It was so good that I had to make her leave before I caved.

The second she closed the door, I almost shoved her panties in my mouth. They smelled so delicious that I growled, pressing down on my aching cock as I tasted the cream she'd left me and hardened all over again. I was hooked on her, completely addicted to all of her, and I didn't ever want to get better.

The rest of the day was beyond torture, and every time I felt like I might die, I played with that app and killed her with me. I pictured what she must look like — if she lay spread out or with her legs clenched together, if she was moaning quietly or loud enough for my neighbors to hear. I pictured her naked and sprawled out on my bed, twitching every time I changed the settings, touching herself because she simply couldn't help it. I pictured her coming without permission and the things I'd do to her ass if she did.

By the time I walked into the house, my legs were shaking, but that was nothing compared to her. She was covered in sweat, hair matted to her forehead and thighs spread, trembling as she gripped the couch around her. It looked a little like she was about to give birth — a visual that was attempting to derail what I wanted to do — and I stripped off my clothes before I reached her. "My beautiful, perfect girl. You miss me?"

I slapped her thick thigh and dropped down to taste her pussy, pulling that vibe out of her and letting it drop to the ground.

"Tobias Novak, I swear to God—"

I shut her up with my tongue, but I knew what she needed. She needed to be fucked into oblivion before she cried, and I was beyond ready to oblige. The moment I felt like I'd gotten enough of her taste to tide me over, I sank deep inside her, catching her in a heated, drawn-out kiss before I broke it to give in to both of our desires. I fucked her hard and fast, filling the house with the sound of our skin slapping together and our needy groans.

I had no intention of stopping, not until Nila came so many times she slumped, and after three of them I could tell she wasn't done. I bottomed out, grinding myself against her as I filled her ear with filth, describing to her how I'd had her soaked panties in my mouth when she left me earlier. That alone was enough to drag a fourth orgasm from her. I pulled out completely, letting her see how wet my cock was with her come, and then flipped her over to thrust back inside. "Two more, sweetheart."

Her cuss was satisfying, just not as satisfying as the begging that came after those two orgasms, and when she slumped with a whimper, I knew my girl was finally well taken care of.

Only then did I let my eyes close and focus on how wet she was, how hot her pussy felt wrapped around my cock, how slippery it was from how many times she'd come for me. For *me,* not anyone else. *Me,* my cock, my fingers, my words. My girl. I grabbed her hips roughly and pinned her to me as I bottomed out and rutted deeper, coming hard and letting her feel every throb of my cock as I emptied fully inside of her.

I spent the rest of the night spoiling her. I bathed her, dressed her in my clothes, rubbed her shoulders as I whispered praise and how much I loved her into her ear, and when she fell asleep in my arms I held her close the entire night.

It was everything we needed and more.

EIGHTEEN

Birthday Sex

NILA

It was hard for me to look back and understand how it had taken us so long to get together. The restraint it had taken, the willful oblivion we'd had to live in, the utter blindness. I felt a little like I'd been slowly raised to the top of a skyscraper then pushed off, but without the fear of splattering — my Toby would never let that happen to me.

So with stolen kisses and whispered promises, I agreed to go to my own birthday party. I hated being the center of attention, which was one of the many, *many* reasons I'd told Toby's brothers no when they'd tried to make me a model, but Toby was … convincing to say the least.

For one day I would put up with it, because I wouldn't be alone.

"Do you think you're finally going to tell them?" I asked in the car on the way over to his mom's house. "About us, I mean."

"Yup. Kale knows by the way, but I'm telling everyone today. I can do it privately if you don't want your family hearing it like it's new news though." He reached over to grab my thigh. "What would you prefer?"

I didn't know what I preferred. Both options sounded like they had the potential to become disastrous, but I was done hiding, done lying, and I didn't want to wait anymore. "Maybe we'll tell everyone together. Come clean to my side and tell yours at the same time. There's no way we could convince your family members not to accidentally let it slip to one of mine."

"You're not wrong. From the group text thread, some of them are already having drinks. You look beautiful by the way. I love you in that color."

I'd gone with white capris and an orange tank top today — not one part of me wanted to test Toby more than necessary. As much as I wanted him to sneak me away somewhere and fuck me with his fingers in my mouth, I didn't want to risk it with *both* of our families nearby. So, I'd gone simpler. Toby, on the other hand … his jeans hugged him just right and although his grey shirt was a little baggy, it teased just enough of his frame to have me practically salivating for him all over again.

"Thanks," I said. "You dress down pretty well, y'know. I love seeing you in normal clothes."

"Normal clothes," he snorted, turning onto his mom's familiar street. "The older I get, the more I hate suits, honestly. I prefer these fucking grey Target t-shirts over everything these days. You love them too,

I've noticed how cuddly you get when I wear them."

"They're soft," I admitted. "And easy to get my hands under."

"Those are definitely perks." He parked, then leaned over to kiss my cheek. "It'll be a good day, promise. And I'm still fucking you here by the way, those capri pants won't stop me."

He got out of the car with a smirk, leaving me to tip my head back and curse the fucking sky. "Why couldn't I have stayed home for my birthday? It's my party and I'll get railed if I want to," I mumbled, sliding out of the car and clearing my throat. "I'm fine. Let's go."

Knowing how I felt about things, Toby wrapped his arm around me to help steady me as we walked in and were immediately swarmed by family. My parents pulled me away from him instantly, wishing me a happy day and asking a million questions about how I felt being thirty-three — as if it were any different than previous years

— and then Clay whistled to get my attention.

He was standing by a table full of presents with Ariel and the baby, Juliet, her best friend, and all of my aunts and uncles. I might not have noticed anyone else at all if Kale hadn't tripped over those presents and sent three others tumbling to the ground. "Oops. Happy birthday, Nila."

He attempted to shrink back into the background, but seeing as he was the largest one there, it was impossible. Toby shook his head like he wasn't surprised at all, and I walked over to hug each of them in turn.

In true Vaz family fashion, I wasn't allowed to touch the presents until everyone had eaten food and cake, but the biggest surprise of the party came when the Novaks got up on a makeshift stage in the backyard to play me the Happy Birthday song.

Toby pulled me in and held me, not caring at all who was watching, and the second they finished he made his way up there to grab the microphone from Kai. "Nila and I want to say thank you for making today extra special for her. We also have something else we'd like to say. Can you come here, sweetheart?"

My stomach dropped so fast I nearly threw up, but I knew what he was doing, and I was ready to get it over with. I smiled sheepishly at my Aunt Monica and Uncle Richard as I climbed up onto the stage and joined Toby, then leaned up to kiss his cheek. "I'm here."

"I know." He smiled, less comfortable with a microphone than his brothers, but still miles better than I was. "Nila and I are together, and I know for half of you that feels weird to hear, but for the longest time we were only friends. I went to her family parties as her boyfriend so she wouldn't be drilled about being single, but in all that pretend, we found something raw and real and discovered that it was never actually pretend for us. We're in love."

"I fucking knew it!" Uncle Richard yelled, earning a slap to the shoulder and a hushed scolding from his wife. "Don't give me that, Monica, I told you! No way those two were screwing before."

At least two people whistled and Toby laughed it off and pulled me in for a kiss, only breaking it to smile as our families cheered. When his mother ran up with tears in her eyes, I almost joined her. She pulled me in for a tight hug, letting me know I'd always been family and how happy she was for us, then tugged on her son's ear happily. "How long did you keep this from me?"

Toby managed to get out of it when Archie squeezed between them to get to me, and I bit my lip with a smile as he hugged me. "Looks like you were right again, Arch. Is there something you wanna tell us? About a crystal ball, maybe?"

"Nope. My sorcery is all done behind closed doors, but I will say that Sage is probably next."

"Focus on your own love life, Bror. We're all fine," Toby squeezed his shoulder in a way that only a big brother could get away with, but Archie was completely unfazed.

"I'll worry about mine when my family is all settled," he said. "I'm the most patient one here."

Toby looked as though he wanted to argue but thought better of it, so I did it for him. "I don't know, Arch. Tobias waited for me for years. I'd say he's pretty patient."

"Yeah, he is." He smiled knowingly, looking older than he was, and then moved so the twins could get their hugs in.

"Just want all of you to know that I knew about it first. Someone write down how special I am to Toby please." Kale pulled me into his chest and squeezed, letting go when his mom slapped the back of his head as Toby was reaching to pull him off of me.

JENSEN

I couldn't stop myself from laughing a little too loudly at them, but I felt … light. Happy, truly happy, for the first time since before Jackie's accident. I had no secrets, nothing weighing me down. Just a giant family that got even bigger with this news.

Both sides spoiled me with dancing, a giant, delicious cake, and more presents than I knew what to do with — but I was most curious about Toby's. He bought me a ridiculously gorgeous diamond necklace, which was more than enough on its own, but he told me quickly that it wasn't my real present.

"How the hell is this not considered a real present?"

"You'll see, but *when* you see it all depends on your answer to this next question. Move in my room with me."

I giggled a little. "That didn't sound like a question, T. It sounded like an order."

"Oh, well, I stand by how I said it, but I'll add something else." He touched my chin softly and kissed my nose. "Please."

It wasn't honestly much of a decision. I spent most nights with him anyway since he'd woken up from that nightmare, and I hated the nights we did spend alone. "Of course, T. You could've skipped the bling and just gone with that, you know. Best present I've gotten all day." I kissed him deeply, wrapping my arms around his neck and rocking up on my toes, shivering slightly as his hands slid along my hips and around to my lower back.

"That wasn't your present either. You'll get it soon though. Just a little late. Plus, you look good in bling. Come here." He took my hand and led me up the stairs, and I followed like a dog in heat.

The presents, the promises, the scent of his cologne as it wafted down behind him … I needed him. "Where are we going?"

"My room, and no, this isn't another present for you. This one is for me." He glanced back to wink at me, sending a little shiver down my spine as we walked into his old room and shut the door.

"Then do tell, Tobias. How can I thank you for a great day?"

"You can let me taste you right here on my old bed, then swallow every drop of my come on your knees."

I'd never get used to hearing him talk to me like that. Toby, my best friend, the respectful, wonderful man who had been by my side and protected me … I'd never get over hearing him say those things. "Then lock the door." I stripped my lower half as he locked us in, then laid back and spread out on the mattress with my fingers dancing down my stomach toward my pussy. "Wet for you, T. Always."

"No touching, I want it all."

He lapped up my inner thigh in a way that made me gasp, but it was nothing compared to his tongue sliding inside my pussy for more. I wrapped my hands around my thighs and pulled my legs up, splaying them as much as I could as I craned my neck to watch him. It was so hard to keep quiet, not to scream for him, moan for him, die for him and that silver, filthy tongue, but when he reached up to shove two fingers into my mouth I lost that battle. Luckily for us it was muffled, because the second he sucked my clit into his mouth, I came with a shocked yell and started sucking his fingers as I rode his face through it.

He pinned me when his other fingers slid into my pussy and pressed down. It was obvious he wanted more from me, and it didn't take him long to get it — he had me so turned on, feeling so fucking high for him that I had no control over that second orgasm at all. It seemed to never end. Every little movement he made kept me riding that ledge, until I was shaking and weak and so desperate to return the favor that I'd have done just about anything to please him.

"Sir," I mumbled around his fingers. "Let me."

He sat up and wiped his face, sucking his fingers into his mouth before fumbling with his slacks. "Got me throbbing, sweetheart."

I grinned and rolled onto my back, then let my head fall over the side of the bed as I spread my legs for him to give him a good view. "If I can still breathe during this, I'll think you're holding out on me."

His sneer sent a chill up my spine. "Loud and clear, Niles. Open."

He pushed his fat cock into my throat, and I settled my hands on his thighs in case I needed to tap out, though I knew I wouldn't. I could do this for him, at least once.

Deeper and deeper he slid until I couldn't move my head at all — couldn't nod, couldn't bob, couldn't breathe, and it had me curling my toes and rocking my hips again. "Gods, I remember wondering how deep my best friend would take my cock. Now I know. Throat was made for me."

All of me was made for you. What's yours is yours, T.

He slapped my pussy, whispering how good I looked under him like this and completely at his mercy, and I focused on nothing but that hard, hot cock until he started fingering me again. This time, he didn't hold back. I could hear the evidence of how wet I was splashing around his fingers and alternating with the sound of my own gagging, and the combination had me moaning around him and squirting all over his fingers, all over the bed, making me lightheaded and dizzy until I heard the words I was desperate to hear:

"Ah fuck, I'm gonna come." Toby gripped my throat with his come-covered hand and bottomed out, stretching my jaw and blocking my nose until my chest was heaving and I was sure I was going to die — but the moment he was done, he pulled out and dropped down to kiss all over my face.

I barely heard the praises that fell from his lips, but I knew what he was saying. I was his good girl, his *duktig flicka,* and he'd never stop making me feel this good.

It was the best birthday I'd ever had.

NINETEEN

One Fort at a Time

The only thing worse than a work meeting was an emergency Saturday work meeting. Someone was attempting to sue us for not giving them enough work, but after two hours of going through their contract, we discovered they had no grounds to stand on. They did, however, breach their contract by starting this whole thing, so with that we all parted ways, happy it hadn't escalated into something worse.

Normally, I'd never attend these meetings, but since Brennan was C.E.O. now he had asked me to tag along, and my older brother didn't ask for things unless it was important.

As I drove home, I thought of that first morning Nila had officially lived in our house, how I walked in and saw her cooking in her panties. She'd killed me then and every day since, but now that she was actually living in my room with me, I finally got to have her any time I wanted.

Everything between us was exactly how it should have been all along, but even I knew the timing had happened this way for a reason. Because we'd waited, we wouldn't just be each other's partner for a time and then break up like so many young people did. Because we'd waited, we'd be getting married one day. Because we'd waited … we were it for each other.

I walked into my house with a smile that could only have been replaced with lust, which was exactly what happened when I saw her in the kitchen in her panties again, just like I'd daydreamed about. She was painfully gorgeous in simple pink cotton boy shorts, making me harder with each step toward her, because this time I didn't have to stand back and dream. This time, I could have her. "Have I told you today that you're mine?"

"Mmm, I don't think so," she said, tilting her head. "Am I yours?"

I smirked, tugging her head back by her hair and kissing her. "Yes. All of you." I slapped her ass to watch it bounce, then kneeled behind her so I could bury my face in it. "Missed you, booty."

"Did you just talk to my ass like it can hear you?" she asked. "Weirdo."

I nodded so she could feel it. "Don't judge me, your ass and I have our own relationship, we normally talk after you fall asleep."

I kissed it, unable to stop my grin as she wiggled it in my face and reached around to smack my shoulder gently. "Well talk to it later or I swear, I'll put yolks in this omelet."

"You wouldn't dare," I said in mock offense, but I got back to my feet and moved away so she could work. "If I asked you to go have lunch with my mom, would you?"

"Of course, I love Molly. Why do you sound like you're not sure?"

"I don't know. She's probably going to ask for dating advice or something awkward. I'd appreciate it, I hate thinking about how lonely she is at home. Maybe you guys could go out to lunch or something."

Nila set the spatula down and pulled me into a kiss, then nodded as she rubbed my cheek with her thumb. "I've got this. Don't worry, baby. Okay? I'll call her after we eat."

I couldn't stop the grin that overtook my face. "I love you."

It still felt surreal being able to say those words to her, and even more so when she took a deep, slow breath and said them back.

"I love you too, T. And nice save … no yolks for you."

"Wait, what did Snow White name her pet hen?" When she looked at me like I'd lost my mind, I giggled. "It's a joke, guess."

"Um … egg white?" she guessed.

My smile faded. "You heard that one before?"

"No, it's just exactly as ridiculous as you are." Nila kissed me gently and went back to cooking, but I could see the smile playing across her face.

"Alright fine … *omelet* that one slide."

The face she made at the pun had me laughing so hard I coughed, and she dropped my plate on the table unceremoniously before gripping my chin to kiss the hell out of me. "You're insane, Tobias Novak. Absolutely bonkers."

"Bonkers for you."

We ate with her feet in my lap and I rubbed them while she set up lunch plans with my mom. Hearing them talk and knowing we were officially together now had me feeling warm inside, and when my mother enthusiastically said she could be ready in an hour, Nila jumped up and ran to get dressed.

I'd miss her, but I had my own secret motives for wanting her to leave the house. I had a fort to put together. I had been accumulating the stuff for a few weeks, but now that she was all moved into my room, I knew her old room would be perfect for it.

I set up soft-white lights all along the crown molding, covered the ground with the best camping mattresses I could find and pillow top paddings to go with them. I hung up sheets and more lights to help with the aesthetic of the coolest pillow fort I'd ever seen, and bought special blankets and pillows to stay in there all the time, so whenever she needed an escape she could go in there and relax.

I knew it wasn't a conventional birthday gift for a thirty-three-year-old, and the necklace was, but this was something I knew she'd love more than any piece of jewelry. That was just who she was.

I snuck her favorite teddy bear in last, and the second she got back home I went to cover her eyes. I led her there slowly, and although I knew she would love it, I still felt butterflies erupt in my stomach as I opened the door and stood behind her. "Ready for your last birthday gift?"

"Seriously?" she asked excitedly. "Hell yes! What is it?"

I removed the blindfold so she could see for herself. My chest tightened when she gasped loudly and took two quick steps in, then stopped and pivoted like she didn't know where to look first. I watched her clock the radio and the TV, the bookshelf, and she had tears in her eyes when she scooped up her bear and turned to face me again.

"You did all this for me?"

I closed the distance with our gazes locked. "Absolutely. Now we can have fort night whenever we want, we can sleep here sometimes or the bed, and if I ever drive you crazy you can evict me from the fort and unwind with a book or whatever you want. My favorite memories are the ones we spent together in pajamas surrounded by sheets. This is our new fort, and the closet has multiple sets of fresh sheets and blankets. Oh, also a mini fridge."

"We live here now," she said firmly. "Fuck your bedroom. We live here with the lights and the … love." She flung herself at me, hugging me tightly until I lifted her off the ground and carried her back to plop down on the mattress.

"Soft, huh? You'll hear no complaints from me, sweetheart. I'd live anywhere with you."

"It's amazing in here. You're amazing. Can we stay here tonight?" She tugged at my shirt, reaching under it to touch my skin. "Naked this time since we're no longer in the living room with huge windows?"

"It's like you can read my mind. Hell yeah, we can. Want me to order pizza later so we don't even have to leave when we want dinner?"

She nodded quickly, then kissed my beard a couple of times. "Yes, that. I hate not being able to touch you. I feel like I've been starving for you for years and now I can't get enough."

"I know the feeling." I helped her undress, then let her do the same for me as the scent of fresh linen mixed with our own. "I hope you never get enough."

"I won't." She laid me back and looped her leg over me, settling against my chest and relaxing there where she could hear my heartbeat. "You were right, by the way. Molly asked me for dating advice, but I'll spare you the details there. I'm taking her out for drinks next weekend though."

"Drinks?" I let my hand fall to my face and then slid it through my hair. "Should be fun. Am I allowed to come?"

Amusement laced her voice. "If you want to listen to me tell your mom how to rope in a silver fox, then sure. If not … then maybe you just stay here and I'll make it up to you when I get home."

"Gross. I'll just wait here and imagine how many men are looking at your ass so I'm nice and pent up when you get home. How's that sound to you?"

She bit my chest gently. "Promise to spank me?"

"I promise."

I held her there and thought about all the times I'd watched a man buy her a drink, how close I'd been to losing her with every single one, and how she finally saw me the way I'd always seen her.

Our future was just beginning, and we were going to build a good one … one fort at a time.

READY FOR SAGE'S STORY? CHECK OUT "OVER A CLIFF"

THE MILIAS MIX

Can't You See - the Marshall Tucker Band
Gimme Little Sign - Brenton Wood
Can I be him - James Arthur
You're My Best Friend - Queen
All Of Me - John Legend
Going In Circles - Christopher Crius
Shape of You - Ed Sheeran
Everything About You - Avant
Never Gonna Let You Down - Colbie Caillat
You Can Call Me Al - Paul Simon
I Don't Care - Justin Bieber and Ed Sheeran
Criminal - State Champs
Just Gets Better With Time - The Whispers
We Belong Together - Richie Valens
Iris - The Goo Goo Dolls
One Fine Day - The Chiffons
This Magic Moment - The Drifters & Ben E. King
Then He Kissed Me - The Crystals
Tell Him - The Exciters
Maybe Baby - Crickets

LOOKING FOR YOUR NEXT OCTAVIA JENSEN READ?

VISIT
WWW.OCTAVIAJENSEN.COM

Octavia Jensen

VISIT OCTAVIA JENSEN AT

www.octaviajensen.com

Or check her out on social media!

Facebook: Author Octavia Jensen

Instagram: @authoroctaviajensen

TikTok: @authoroctaviajensen